ART AND HISTORY OF
PRAGUE

BONECHI

Distributed by:

NEPALA, spol. s r.o. Horňátecká 1772/19, 182 00 Praha 8, Česká republika
Tel.:+420 284 686 704 - Fax: +420 284 686 606
Mobil: +420 775 368 449 - +420 602 368 449
E-mail: nepala@bonechi.cz - Internet: www.bonechi.cz

Concept and project: Casa Editrice Bonechi
Editorial management: Monica Bonechi
Graphic concept: Monica Bonechi
Graphic design and cover: Manuela Ranfagni
Editing: Federica Balloni
Texts: Giuliano Valdes *with* Federica Balloni *and* Patrizia Fabbri.
Drawing pages. 78-79, map of Prague and the city's districts: Stefano Benini
Drawings pages. 16-17, 24, 58-59, 74-75, 108-109 and inside cover: Sauro Giampaia

Printed in Italy by Centro Stampa Editoriale Bonechi - *Sesto Fiorentino.*

The photographs in this book are the property of the Casa Editrice Bonechi Archives
and were taken by Marco Bonechi *and* Andrea Pistolesi.

Other sources:
© Picture Library of the Prague Castle: *pages 12 top and centre, 17 (the three busts), 24 bottom.*
© Jewish Museum in Prague: *pages. 111 top, 113, 114, 115, 116, 117, 118, 119, 122.*

The photographs on pages 29, 36 bottom and 106 top and centre, courtesy of the National Gallery in Prague.
The photographs on the top of page 40, courtesy of the Order of the Capuchin Friars Minor – Loreto Sanctuary.
*The photographs on pages 31 centre, 37 bottom right, 69 bottom right, 74 left, 79 (statues . 23, 26, 27, 29), 84 top left and right, 105 centre and bottom,
110 bottom left, 112 bottom, 121 centre, 123, 129, 130, 134, and 135 top and bottom right, courtesy of* Anatol Nepala.

The publisher wishes to thank the Order of the Capuchin Friars Minor of the Loreto Sanctuary, *the* Senate of the Czech Republic, *the* Palace Gardens Beneath the Castle , Psalterium s.r.o.,
the W.A. Mozart Museum, *the* National Library of the Czech Republic, *the* Bedřich Smetana Museum, Antonín Dvořák Museum, *the* National Museum of Prague, *the* National Theatre,
the U Fleků Beer Museum and Royal Chapter of Saints Peter and Paul of Vyšehrad, *for their kind and valuable cooperation.*

The publisher apologizes for an errors or omissions of attribution and is ready to compensate parties holding rights to the photographs.

Arte e Storia - PRAGA - n° 54 - Pubblicazione Periodica Trimestrale - Autorizzazione del Tribunale di Firenze n° 3873 del 4/8/1989 - Direttore Responsabile: Giovanna Magi

ISBN 978-88-476-2000-1
www.bonechi.com

INTRODUCTION

"The Magical City", "The Golden City", "The City of a Hundred Towers", the "Paris of the East"; these are just some of the most common definitions adopted by popular tourist publications when describing Prague, a city of around 1,200,000 inhabitants and, since 1st January 1993, capital of the Czech Republic, as well as capital of central Bohemia. The city offers a wealth of architectural, artistic and cultural treasures, and possesses an individual charm: buildings everywhere are of pleasing architectural form and proportional harmony, with close attention to ornamental detail. It lies proudly along the banks of the River Vltava (also know as the Moldau), amid the gentle surroundings of the hills which characterise this part of Bohemia. Prague has been a melting-pot of ethnic groups since ancient times, existing by combining Czech elements with Jewish and German ones, and allowing the development of religious movements, trade and commerce, and industry, thanks to its favourable geographic position on the communication routes between Central and Eastern Europe, and between the North and South of the vast German and Slavonic area. A jealous keeper of its mysteries, the city is reluctant to reveal itself to the curiosity of those wanting to unearth the secrets of the alchemists of the past. The birthplace or one time residence of many famous people, such as the astronomers Tycho Brahe and Johannes Kepler, the Dientzenhofers, Albert Einstein, Wolfgang Amadeus Mozart, Antonín Dvořák, Bedřich Smetana, Jaroslav Hašek, Franz Kafka, Charles IV, Jan Hus, St John Nepomuk, and many other illustrious figures, the city bears witness to cultures and civilisations from all over the world. Over the centuries it has survived wars and disasters. Only in 1968 were the tanks of the Warsaw Pact able to defeat its rebellious nature: the people's and the nation's thirst for freedom was satisfied 20 years after Jan Palach had been engulfed by flames, making him the martyr of a shattered "Spring". The first settlements on the site of the modern city date back to Neolithic times, and fortified settlements were first recorded in the 9th century. Primitive centres joined together around the fortresses of Hradčany and Vyšehrad between the 9th and 10th centuries, and from that time onwards the Přemysl made this the most important castle in Bohemia. As a result it became the focal point for the activities of craftsmen and merchants, attracting mainly Jews and Germans. Having become a Bishop's See in 973, Prague obtained city status between 1232 and 1235. Charles IV then made it the capital of the Empire, founding the University here

A night time view of the Charles Bridge, Malá Strana and the majestic Prague Castle dominating the city.

Prague is also known for the magic of the Moldau and the many bridges linking the two parts of the city which have inspired artists and awed visitors through the centuries. The lively and bustling Charles Bridge is the most famous and connects the Starè Město and Malá Strana districts. A boat ride along the Moldau is an ideal way to enjoy the sights and beauties of the city in summer or winter.

in 1348 and preparing the ground for large scale urban development. In 1419 the followers of Želivský freed the Hussites held prisoner in the New Town Hall, and threw out the Catholic counsellors. This marked the beginning of a long period of religious conflict. In fact, the ascension of the Habsburgs in 1526 marked the decline of Prague, and this became even more marked after the failure of the revolt against the Viennese sovereigns in 1547. While having suffered limitations to its autonomy and the loss of its Court, which had been transferred to Vienna, the city underwent a brief period of revival under Rudolph II who settled here between 1583-1610, and who also contributed to the Germanisation of the city. The Czech revolt of 1618, which began with the "Second Prague Defenestration", led to the Thirty Years' War. Following its defeat in the Battle of White Mountain (8th Nov 1620) Prague entered a period of deep decline from all points of view: the wave of middle-class emigration in the first half

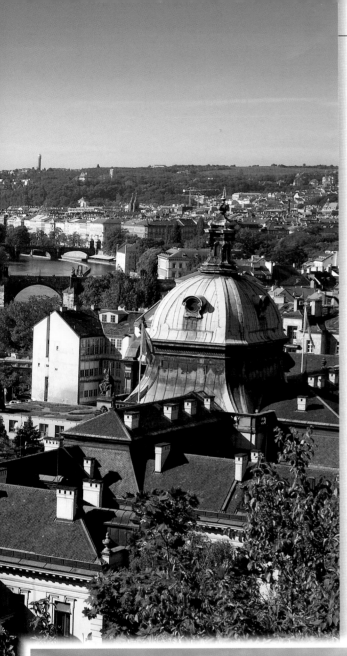

of the 17th century was of biblical proportions. The upris-ings of 1848 failed in their attempt to gain freedom for the Slavs who opposed the centralisation policy introduced by Joseph II. 1861 marked a clear turning-point with the success of the Slavs in the municipal elections.

Between the 19th and 20th centuries the economic and industrial development of Prague led to a considerable influx of the rural population, and caused a growing interest on the part of the nobility in cultural and intellectual pursuits. After the First World War Prague was proclaimed the capital of Czechoslovakia. The city endured the brutal domination of the Nazis from 1939 until 1945 when it was liberated by the Russians. In 1948 a Communist coup d'état transformed Czechoslovakia into a People's Republic, and 1960 marked the birth of the Czechoslovakian Socialist Republic. The long ordeal seemed to be coming to an end in 1968 when the new, more liberal programme adopted by Dubček (the so-called "Prague Spring"), appeared to open the way towards reform and civil liberties. However, the ever-present threat of the Soviet, Communist monolith was brutally felt on 21th August 1968 when tanks were sent into Prague, causing the indignant reaction of its inhabitants, and culminating in the suicides of the students Palach and Zajíc. Twenty years later a protest march was held against the Soviet occupiers to demand liberty and civil rights. Despite police repression, which was repeated a year later to oppose the demands of the "Charta 77" movement, this event later led, through the "Velvet Revolution", to the fall of the Communist Regime in Czechoslovakia and to the resignation of Gustav Husák. Václav Havel took his place and became President of the Republic at the end of 1989. The free elections of 1990 marked the victory of candidates led by Havel and Dubček, the latter having returned to Prague from Slovakia. On 1st January 1993 the division of the Federal Republic of Czechoslovakia was ratified, giving rise to the Czech and the Slovak Republics, with Prague and Bratislava as their respective capitals.

A view of the Moldau, the Charles Bridge and Starè Mĕsto.

The Castle

Pražský hrad

*N*o longer encumbered by its original function as a purely defensive stronghold, today Prague Castle is more like a small town presenting a harmonious appearance, as the various separate components have been quite elegantly unified. The residence of the dukes of Bohemia was situated on this hill as early as the 980s when prince Bořivoj founded the first royal palace here. According to legend, princess Libuše originally foresaw its foundation in a prophetic vision and predicted that a rich and powerful city would arise on this green slope on the river Vltava. It is also said that an ancient Slav place of worship was located here. In any case, St Mary's Church was built here at the end of the 9th century and in about 920 duke Vratislav I also built the church dedicated to St George and consecrated in 925. Not long after, the Rotunda of St Vitus was built by Wenceslas, who would subsequently be assassinated and then too join the glorious ranks of the saints. In the 10th century the Castle was more or less exactly the same size as that of today and an early wooden fortification probably also existed. Fre-

quently besieged and destroyed and just as frequently rebuilt and fortified, the Castle experienced a long period of energetic development from the 12th century when the Přemyslid princes took up residence there. Under Přemysl Otakar I, Wenceslas I and Přemysl Otakar II, despite long periods of war and threats of invasion, the Castle buildings increased and included the Royal Palace, the Romanesque part of which was begun by Soběslav I in the first half of the 12th century; enlarged and modernised in 1252 by the future Otakar II, it was entirely destroyed by a storm in 1280. Under Wenceslas II and his son Wenceslas III, repair and restoration work was only slowly undertaken. An unfortunate period followed under John of Luxembourg and the Castle was neglected, but during the mid 14th century, his son, Charles IV, who had been educated at the court of France, built a new Royal Palace and Cathedral worthy of the newly flourishing city, thus bringing a sophisticated and previously unknown splendour to the Castle. In turn his son, Wenceslas IV, continued and extended his father's achievements. A series of rulers followed who were more interested in wars than in improving the capital of

the kingdom until finally Vladislav II Jagellonsky turned his attention to the Castle at the start of the 16th century. He was responsible for the new fortifications but also for a series of new buildings and plans. With the arrival of Ferdinand I, a member of the Hapsburg family (1526-1564), it was decided that the Castle required a new look and character, more suited to the requirements of an important court: gardens were created, buildings were enlarged and its magnificence increased. The devastating fire of 1541 made radical rebuilding urgent and also facilitated the work of improvement and development instigated by first Maximilian II and then Rudolph II (an art lover and enthusiast of the sciences), who enriched the Castle with both his numerous collections and his illustrious scholarly guests, such as Tycho de Brahe and Kepler. In the early 17th century under Ferdinand II the Baroque was splendidly introduced to the Castle and its gardens. The style continued to develop under Ferdinand III, Leopold I (who laid the first stone of the Cathedral's Baroque completion in 1673) and Charles VI. Finally, in the mid 18th century, Maria Theresa of Austria commissioned the court architect, Nicola Pacassi, to plan and carry out the definitive appearance and arrangement of the general structure. The Castle then fell into a kind of oblivion, only interrupted by sporadic and sumptuous coronation ceremonies. Impoverished by expropriations and damaged by extensive military use of its buildings, it came to life once more under Ferdinand V who chose it as his personal residence, and its role was once again reasserted in the 20th century when the Republic came into being. The Castle was chosen as the natural residence for the President and was restored and adapted for its new purpose by Josip Plečnik. More recently Václav Havel initiated the restoration of many rooms and areas that had for long been neglected and inaccessible; returned once more to their original splendour, these are now open to the public.

Two glimpses of the city dominated by the majestic Castle.

The main entrance to the Castle from the Hradčanské náměstí.

Below, together with the official corps, the mighty stone colossi guard the elaborate Giants' Gate, named after them (right).

Giants' Gate

Clearly Hapsburg in style, the name of the gate is derived from the *gigantic figures* which dominate the pillars at the entrance, designed by I. Platzer the Elder and made between 1770 and 1771. All along the railings on either side of the gate, are more statues portraying cherubs, an eagle, (a symbol of the Hapsburg rulers), and a lion (animal symbolizing the kingdom of Bohemia), forming a varied series of contemporary works, also by Ignác Platzer. The figures seen here today are copies however, as the originals, made of sandstone that is badly affected by climatic conditions, were removed and replaced at the beginning of the 20th century.

FIRST COURTYARD

The Castle Gate leads into the Ceremonial Court-yard (or First Courtyard). This is located where once there was a deep ravine dividing the district of Hradčany from the older buildings of the Castle, and only crossed by bridges. This court was also built during the Hapsburg period (1763-1771) when Maria Theresa of Austria instructed the court architect Nicola Picassi,

assisted by the master builder A. Lurago, to design this great square where the pre-existing gully had been filled in. To give the square an elegant appearance the architect created three fine buildings in the Viennese style, forming a majestic U shape. Thus the concept of the defensive fortress was clearly abandoned and the appearance of the Castle began to evolve into that of an airy imperial residence. This continued with the construction of the New Palace which would later be extended with the addition of the buildings that surround the Second Court-yard. The halls, apartments and rooms of the **North** and **South Wings** are still used for state visits, while the **West Wing** is generally used for official receptions and events.

TOMÁŠ GARRIGUE MASARYK

Prague Castle and its many streets and alleys have a long and crowded history. Standing at the entrance is one of the many tangible signs of this splendid past: the elegant statue of Tomáš Garrigue Masaryk (1850-1937), an important symbol of more recent Czech history. Renowned as the first president of the Republic of Czechoslovakia, which came into being in 1918, Masaryk's offices were located in the Castle and he was responsible for commissioning the innovative Slovenian architect, Plečnik, to work on the Castle and, with masterly skill transform it into a palace suitable for the representation of government.

Matthias' Gate

Preceded by two lofty flag staffs 25 metres high, originally made from the trunk of a single fir tree from Moravia, wedged between the buildings of the West Wing the 17th-century Matthias' Gate leads to the Second Courtyard. Like a solitary triumphal arch, it was erected by Matthias II in 1614 (and is therefore much earlier than the buildings that surround it) in early Baroque style though with Rudolphesque influences, it was probably the work of the court architect, Giovanni Maria Filippi, though it has also been suggested that the design was by Scamozzi. It is clearly a commemorative structure: engraved at the top are the titles and heraldic emblem of Emperor Matthias, while below, beneath the cornice, are the numerous coats of arms of the countries in his domain. Access to the various rooms of the splendid West Wing is from here, via the two stairways that lead out of the entrance way.

The sandstone Matthias Gate once stood alone, like a triumphal arch.

THE CHANGING OF THE GUARD

For centuries a small group of guards has protected the safety of the castle. Though today they wear elegant modern uniforms newly designed in 1989 by Theodor Pištěk, life was rather more difficult in the past in particular in the 18th century when, only paid with free lodging and wood for their fires for warmth, they were reduced to only 24 men armed with barely three bullets

each. The institution of the castle guards survived, however, and even now every day on the hour from 5 in the morning until 11 pm the changing of the guard is performed in front of the gates. The most spectacular of these ceremonies however, takes place at midday under the eyes of an admiring public, complete with brass fanfares and the exchange of flags.

The second courtyard with the fountain and the well; on the right the North Gate that leads to the Renaissance gardens.

SECOND COURTYARD

Older than the preceding court (its construction began in the 15ᵗʰ century), and also built over a pre-existing moat that enclosed and protected the Romanesque city walls, the Second Courtyard was surrounded by buildings in different styles, from different periods and with different purposes, often also quite separate and independent from each other. It was only with the 18ᵗʰ-century project of Pacassi that the courtyard assumed a harmonious and unified aspect. Newly paved during the 1970s, in the centre of the court stands an elegant Baroque **fountain** designed with a mythological theme by Francesco Torre in 1686 and decorated by the sculptor Jeronym Kohl. Nearby is an old **well**, for long a fundamental source for supplying water, which was decorated in the 18ᵗʰ century with an unusual net-like design in wrought iron to crown it, reminiscent of a birdcage. In the past, close by and joined to the West Wing, was the oldest Castle church, the renowned St Mary's church which dated from as early as the 9ᵗʰ century.

NORTH WING: RUDOLPH GALLERY AND SPANISH HALL

An enthusiastic collector, principally of works of art and especially paintings, Emperor Rudolph II created a vast and rare collection and commissioned G. Gargiolli to design the most suitable setting possible for it in the stable block - the splendid **Rudolph Gallery**. As time passed, however,

Shots of the magnificent Spanish Gallery, one of the most important in the entire Castle and, above, the adjacent Gallery of Rudolph II.

the prestigious imperial collection seemed destined to be dismantled. However, today's gallery, opened in 1965, is still based on the original nucleus of precisely the imperial collections of Rudolph and boasts masterpieces by Paolo Veronese, Rubens, Titian and Tintoretto, flanked by more recent paintings from the 18th, 19th and 20th centuries by artists of Prague. Just as interesting, and designed by G. M. Filippi, is the enormous **Spanish Hall**, originally built between 1602 and 1606, but refurbished several times in the 18th and 19th centuries giving it the clearly Baroque appearance remaining today. Also furnished to house the collections of the emperor, it gradually assumed a purely formal role hosting court celebrations and balls.

Left, the lavish interior of the Chapel of the Holy Cross and a detail of the outside.

Chapel of the Holy Cross

In the south-east area of the Second Courtyard is the simple and elegant Chapel of the Holy Cross, built by A. Lurago between 1758 and 1763 according to a design by Nicola Pacassi. However, all that remains of that period are the high altar made by Ignác Platzer and a *Crucifix* painted by S. Balko.

All the rest of the building dates from the 19th century restoration, resulting from the need to adapt the building to its role as a private chapel for the emperor.

The elegant Third Courtyard with the Old Provost's House, the Cathedral of St Vitus and a wing of the Royal Palace.

Below, the equestrian statue of Saint George, patron of soldiers and knights. This is a copy of the fourteenth century bronze statue that now stands inside the Royal Palace.

THIRD COURTYARD

An entrance set into the Central wing, where robust remains of the Romanesque fortifications can still be seen, leads into the heart of the Castle, the large third courtyard, originally on two levels that were merged during the 20th century by the spectacular paving in granite by Plečnik. Modern and old features mingle harmoniously in this area, with the Cathedral towering above. Archaeological excavations have for long investigated the historical and architectural history of the original nucleus of the Castle here. The **Old Provost's House**, built on the site of the Romanesque Bishop's palace of which an original window survives, is flanked by a many modern and linear granite **monoliths**.

CATHEDRAL OF ST VITUS
Chrám sv. Víta

The history of Prague Cathedral, the true spiritual centre of the entire country, is lengthy and complex. In 925, where this impressive monument now stands, St Wenceslas built the small circular Romanesque structure of St Vitus, his future burial place, flanked not long afterwards by the bishops' residence and subsequently replaced in 1060 by a new basilica with three naves and two choirs. It was not until 1344 that Charles IV commissioned the French architect, Mathieu d'Arras, to build a new Gothic cathedral for the rapidly growing city, which had recently become an archbishopric – a cathedral that would be worthy of housing the body of such a great sovereign as St Wenceslas, the country's patron. The foundation stone was laid on 21 November of that year and the great French cathedrals provided the model for the construction. When Mathieu d'Arras died the work was continued, under the guidance and direct control of Charles IV, by the Swabian architect and sculptor, Petr Parléř, one of the fathers of European Gothic, until his death in 1399. His sons, Jan and Wenceslas, took over but work was interrupted in the 1420s by the Hussite wars. At the time, most of the bell tower had been built but not even half of the building was completed, and the choir was closed with a wall forming a kind of temporary façade so that religious services could be held. The ambulatory and a first Renaissance dome were built in the second half of the 16th century. Thus the Cathedral remained unfinished, with a truncated appearance – the nave barely begun beyond the transept. A series of disastrous events then followed: in 1541 there was a dreadful fire, in 1620 it was pillaged by the Calvinists, a century later it was severely attacked and damaged by the Prussians, and in 1760 lightning struck causing another fire as well as destroying the only existing tower at the time. The work of building the west nave did not then begin until 1872 when Joseph Mocker's project continued the work in complete harmony with the monumental style already existing. When Mocker died, Kamil Hilbert took over in 1899 and in 1929, one thousand years after the death of St Wenceslas, the Cathedral, with its imperious stature and interwoven buttresses so characteristic of the most perfect Gothic architecture, could finally be said to be finished.

The splendid apse, decorated with spires and pinnacles, is illuminated by stained glass windows and surrounded by chapels in the French Gothic style.

The awe-inspiring main façade of the Cathedral of St Vitus.

THE CENTRAL DOORWAY

A 20th century work in bronze, the doorway is composed of ten bas-relief scenes illustrating the history of the Cathedral (O. Španiel, 1927-1929) surmounted by a pediment in sandstone (K. Dvořák, 1939).

CHRIST ON THE CROSS

Made by F. Bílek in 1899, the figure is above a wooden altar by the same artist (1927) and is one of the finest works of modern art in the Cathedral.

Pediment with the Crucifixion, the disputation over Christ's clothes and the deposition.

St Wenceslas receives the body of St Vitus

Charles IV delivers the body of St Vitus to the archbishop

Building the St Vitus Rotunda

Charles IV with his son in the workshop of Petr Parléř

The burial of St Vitus in the Rotunda

Mathieu d'Arras building the Cathedral

The foundation of the basilica

V. M. Pešina and the completion of the Cathedral

The consecration of the basilica

The consecration of the Cathedral

STAINED GLASS WINDOWS BY MUCHA

The Cathedral is illuminated with splendid and glowing stained glass windows that include wonderful masterpieces in the Art Nouveau style by Alfons Mucha.

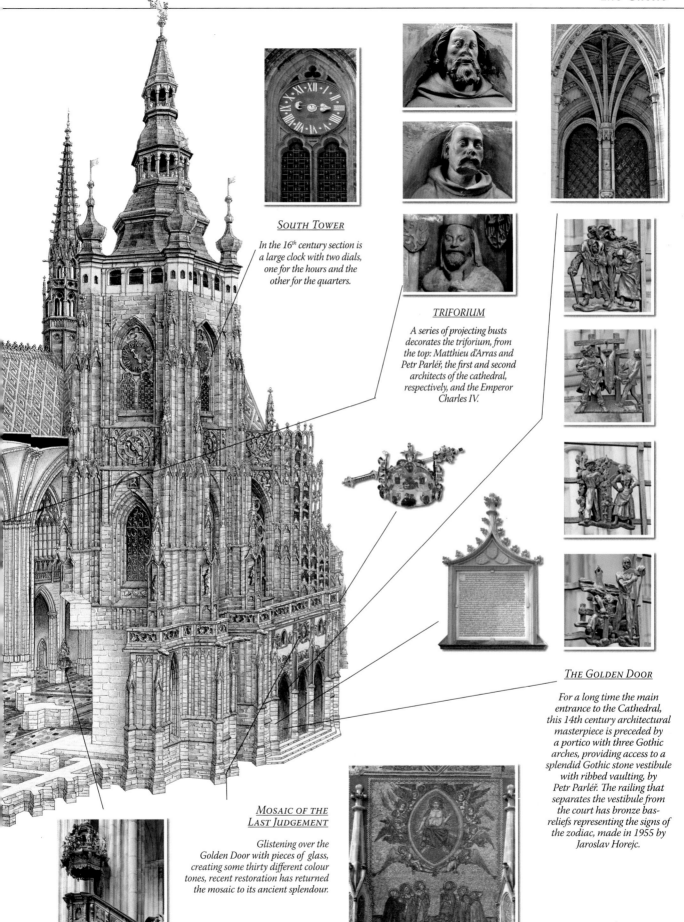

SOUTH TOWER

In the 16th century section is a large clock with two dials, one for the hours and the other for the quarters.

TRIFORIUM

A series of projecting busts decorates the triforium, from the top: Matthieu d'Arras and Petr Parléř, the first and second architects of the cathedral, respectively, and the Emperor Charles IV.

THE GOLDEN DOOR

For a long time the main entrance to the Cathedral, this 14th century architectural masterpiece is preceded by a portico with three Gothic arches, providing access to a splendid Gothic stone vestibule with ribbed vaulting, by Petr Parléř. The railing that separates the vestibule from the court has bronze bas-reliefs representing the signs of the zodiac, made in 1955 by Jaroslav Horejc.

MOSAIC OF THE LAST JUDGEMENT

Glistening over the Golden Door with pieces of glass, creating some thirty different colour tones, recent restoration has returned the mosaic to its ancient splendour.

Elaborate scenes from the Passion of Christ decorate the lunettes above the central door.

Below, details of some of the bas-relief sculptures on the door.

West façade

Framed by two lofty *twin towers* ending in soaring spires (82 metres high, compared to the 99,6 of the south tower), the 20th-century façade has three sections formed by spires, statues and elegant neo-Gothic decorative elements, including the traditional gargoyles, and is dominated by the large rose window designed between 1925 and 1927 by František Kysela. Lower down, three elaborate but elegant entrances with bas-reliefs portraying scenes from the life of St Wenceslas (on the left) and St Adalbert (on the right) and events during the construction of the Cathedral (in the centre), provide access to the well-lit nave.

South façade

This side is almost considered to be the main entrance to the great Cathedral and indeed for centuries it was the only one to provide access. The 14th century south façade is embellished with the magnificent **Golden Door**, crowned by a mosaic of the *Last Judgement*, made about 1370. The three arches of the entrance lead to the renowned and beautifully decorated stone vestibule. On the right, a spiral staircase enclosed by a splendid stone shell, artistically engraved, leads to the external triforium. On the left, and even more impressive, is the *south tower*, raised to a height of more than 50 metres by Petr Parléř but only finished two centuries later with the elegant gilded grating, the clock with two faces, the 16-17th century bells (the largest is nicknamed Sigismund), and ending in a dome redesigned by Nicola Pacassi in Baroque style.

Views of the south façade of the Cathedral, showing the impressive tower crowned by a baroque cupola.

A detail of the gleaming mosaic of Last Judgement above the Golden Door.

The lofty central nave of the Cathedral, enhanced with unusual interlacing in the vault, the glowing rose window, and the brightly coloured stained glass windows in the apse.

The interior

Some 124 metres long, just over 33 high, 60 metres at the widest point of the transept, with two lower naves flanking the central one, the interior of St Vitus' Cathedral is austere, unadorned and harmonious. Light filters through the large stained glass windows and below these, with a height of about 14 metres, runs an elegant and original ambulatory, known as the **internal triforium or arcade**, decorated with a magnificent gallery of sculptures. Below is a long sequence of **chapels**, some of which are antique and were designed by Mathieu d'Arras and Petr Parléř, some of which are more recent. Overhead is the spectacular, uninterrupted interlacing of the meshed pattern in the **vaults**, a genuine innovation in 14th century Europe and once more created by the genius of Petr Parléř. On the west side is the kaleidoscopic colour effect of the **stained glass window**;

27,000 pieces of coloured glass form scenes from the *Creation*. Occupying the centre of the nave is the *burial place of St Adalbert*, for whom a chapel was first built on the exterior of the provisional west façade of the unfinished Cathedral, though this was later destroyed when building work began once more. On the east side is the transept which crosses the nave more or less at the point where building of the Cathedral was interrupted in the 15th century. Standing guard at the majestic intersection of nave and transept are eight wooden statues of the patron saints of Bohemia: Adalbert, John of Nepomuk, Ludmilla, Norbert, Procopius, Sigismund, Wenceslas and Vitus.

The north part of the transept ends in a magnificent Renaissance tribune which was originally used as a monumental and temporary closure for the choir in the unfinished

Above and right, the splendid modern stained glass windows by Alfons Muchas (1860-1939) universally acknowledged as one of the greatest masters of the Art Nouveau style. Below, details of some of the other magnificent stained glass windows that embellish the cathedral.

Cathedral (it was transferred here in 1924), now finished with an 18th-century organ. The south end is lit by a glistening neo-Gothic *stained glass window*, the panes of which represent scenes from the *Universal Judgment*, made in 1939 by Max Švabinský. Lit by three large windows of 20th-century stained glass is the grand *apse*, preceded by the impressive **royal mausoleum** made by the Hapsburgs at the end of the 16th century, where the reclining figures of Ferdinand I, his wife, Anna Jagellonsky and their son, Maximilian II are visible behind

ST. JOANNES BAPT

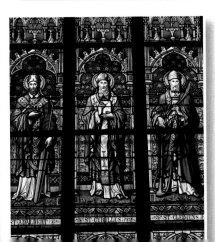

The elegant Chapel of St Sigismund designed by Petr Parléř contains the remains of Sigismund, king of the Burgundians Bohemia

The tomb of St Vitus with the nineteenth century sandstone statue by Emanuel Max.

the statue of the *Risen Christ*. Made by Alexander Collin between 1570 and 1589, this grandiose marble monument is a magnificent conclusion to the **royal crypt** below. Reached from the Chapel of the Holy Cross and rebuilt in the first half of the 20th century, various members of the imperial family have been interred here, behind an elegant enclosure, since the late 16th century.

One of the wooden relief carvings behind the choir stalls; this one depicts the Flight of Frederick the Elector Palatine from Prague; the carving, by Gaspare Becheteler antedates 1630.

The Chapels

There are some 19 chapels in the Cathedral, from the nave to the apse and the south tower. All are splendid and some more grandiose than others. The **Chapel of St Sigismund** is an architectural work by Petr Parléř. The **Chapel of St John the Baptist**, originally an

The statue of Cardinal Bedřich Schwarzenberg, archbishop of Prague (1892-1895), by J. V. Myslbek, stands in front of the Pernštejn Chapel.

The magnificent silver funerary monument to Saint John of Nepomuk by J.E. Fischer von Erlach (1733-1737), is framed by an elegant baldachin and dominated by the figure of the kneeling saint holding a crucifix.

old structure but rebuilt in the 19th century, houses the Gothic tombs of princes Bořivoj II and Boleslav II as well as the 16th century tombs of archbishops Antonín Brusa of Mohelnice and Martin Medek. The **Chapel of the Virgin Mary** was commissioned to be built by Charles IV on the spot where the foundation stone of the Cathedral was laid, and is opposite the *tomb of St Vitus*. Among the oldest in Europe, in the **Chapel of the Holy Reliquaries** are the magnificent sepulchres of Přemysl Otakar I and Přemysl Otakar II, whose burial crown, imperial orb and sceptre have been discovered. But the most beautiful, famous and frequently visited is without doubt the **Chapel of St Wenceslas**, on the east side of the south tower, corresponding to the apse of the old Romanesque rotunda, commissioned by Charles IV and built by Petr Parléř who completed it in 1367.

THE ROTUNDA

Archaeological excavations carried out below the Cathedral of St Vitus today have brought to light the interesting and highly important remains of what was the ancient **pre-Romanesque rotunda of St Vitus** and the early **Romanesque basilica** with its original altar. The discovery is of great historic importance and also provides an extremely evocative access to the neighbouring **royal crypt** where lie the bodies of Charles IV, flanked by his four wives, Wenceslas IV with his wife Joanna of Bavaria, Ladislaus Posthumus and Jiří of Poděbrady. Other members of the imperial family buried here include Emperor Rudolph II, in a rare 17th century coffin made from tin.

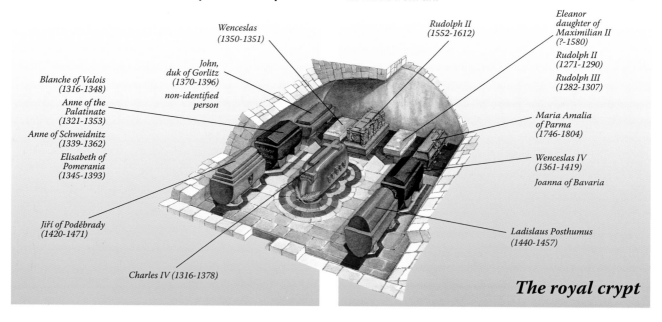

Wenceslas (1350-1351)

John, duk of Gorlitz (1370-1396)

non-identified person

Rudolph II (1552-1612)

Eleanor daughter of Maximilian II (?-1580)

Rudolph II (1271-1290)

Rudolph III (1282-1307)

Blanche of Valois (1316-1348)

Anne of the Palatinate (1321-1353)

Anne of Schweidnitz (1339-1362)

Elisabeth of Pomerania (1345-1393)

Maria Amalia of Parma (1746-1804)

Wenceslas IV (1361-1419)

Joanna of Bavaria

Jiří of Poděbrady (1420-1471)

Ladislaus Posthumus (1440-1457)

Charles IV (1316-1378)

The royal crypt

The Cathedral Treasury and the Crown Jewels

The Cathedral of St Vitus houses and preserves priceless antique treasures of gold and silverwork. Some of these belong to the **Cathedral Treasury**, precious liturgical items dated from the 6th to 20th centuries housed alongside the **New Sacristy** on the north side of the Cathedral. Also located here is the **Old Sacristy**, formerly the Chapel of St Michael, crowned by a vault with an amazing network of ribbing that creates an original hanging keystone. Equally splendid are the **Crown Jewels**, housed in the **Crown Room** above St Wenceslas Chapel, reached from a stairway and protected by a door closed with seven locks. All the jewels are of immense value, including *St Wenceslas sword*, the *Gold Crown*, also named after the saint, dating from the time of Charles IV (according to legend, it is quite dangerous as it is reputed to cause the death of anyone who wears it without any right, within a year), the *sceptre* and the *imperial pommel* from the time of Ferdinand I.

Cathedral Treasury. Silver reliquary of St Vitus, one of six commissioned by king Vladislav Jagellonsky for the Cathedral (late 15th century).

Cathedral Treasury. St Adalbert reliquary.

Crown Jewels. The imperial orb.

Crown Jewels. St Wenceslas' Crown.

Chapel of St Wenceslas

The Chapel has a square plan, is larger in size than the other chapels and is also more sophisticated with almost 1,350 semi-precious stones set into the walls creating a grandiose frame for the fresco cycle dedicated to the *Passion of Christ* (1372-1373). This chapel is, moreover, the most sacred as it houses the relics of prince Wenceslas, patron saint of Bohemia, on the same spot where they were originally buried, in what was then the St Vitus rotunda.

A fine door leads to the stairway up to the Crown Room. Higher up, the chapel has a second fresco cycle, dated 16th-17th century and representing scenes from the life of St Wenceslas. The chapel also contains an unusual tower-shaped reliquary and an excellent painted stone statue of the saint (1373), probably by a nephew of Petr Parléř, standing against the background of another fresco with angels and saints.

The Chapel of Saint Wenceslas with its fine frescoes, and above a detail showing the tabernacle.

The exterior of the Vladislav Hall, the stronghold of the old Royal Palace; below, the ancient passage linking the Cathedral to the Royal Palace.

of 1541 it was Ferdinand I of Hapsburg who had to tackle the problem of the serious damage caused, at the same time rebuilding the Hall of the Diets. As time passed, however, the palace gradually ceased to be used for its original function, first losing its role as a residence for the royal family (the Hapsburgs in fact preferred the rooms in the western part of the castle) while the administrative function was greatly reduced, though it continued to fulfil a role as the setting for important public ceremonies. Lastly, as part of the project for radically rebuilding the entire castle carried out in the 18th century by Nicola Pacassi and commissioned by Empress Maria Theresa, the façades were all modified to achieve an appearance in complete harmony with the surrounding buildings and the old Royal Palace was thus definitively integrated with the new Hapsburg image of this imposing complex.

THE ROYAL PALACE
Královský palác

From the Royal Oratory of the Cathedral a covered passage leads directly to the old Royal Palace, on the south side of the Third Courtyard. The building came into being in the 12th century when prince Soběslav I had the first royal residence built here in Romanesque style and with a rectangular plan. The massive south walls of the palace also became part of the Castle defences. In 1185 the Chapel of All Saints was constructed alongside and in the middle of the 13th century, Přemysl Otakar II had the palace enlarged. It was not until the 14th century when Charles IV was still only the hereditary prince, that the building was significantly enlarged towards the north and the west, thus acquiring space to create the large reception rooms, and the Gothic style was supplanted by the Romanesque. When Wenceslas IV in turn decided that rebuilding was required, he intended to transform the palace into a comfortable and elegant residence for the royal family, though he also extended the buildings and modified the direct passage between the palace and Chapel of All Saints. Due to the Hussite wars the palace was for long abandoned and it was king Vladislav Jagellonsky who restored it to its regal function and status, financing a series of impressive building projects involving in particular the first floor and especially the creation of the attractive Vladislav Hall. After the disastrous fire

The interior

Preceded by the graceful *Eagle Fountain* (1664, made by Francesco Torre), access to the old Royal Palace is through a resplendent 18th century façade and the effect is not unlike travelling back through history. In many of the rooms, halls and stairways it feels almost as though time has stood still. First is the **Green Room**, where at first Charles IV supervised the discussion of minor legal problems and later a fully fledged court tribunal was established at the beginning of the 16th century. Nearby is the first majestic example of the rebuilding carried out by Vladislav Jagellonsky – the huge and spectacular **Vladislav Hall**, commissioned from Benedikt Ried by Vladislav Jagellonsky and replacing three earlier Gothic rooms (including the Throne Room) dating from the time of Charles IV. Some 62 metres long, 16 metres wide and 13 metres high, built between 1492 and 1502 it was the largest room in Europe at the time – large enough indeed to house, as well as the usual ceremonies, equestrian tournaments and even a market. The Hall was greatly admired, especially for the extraordinary design of the groins and the highly elegant 'star-shaped' curved vault and the excellent light provided by the large windows clearly of early Renaissance inspiration. The entire structure is in fact pervaded by a sensation of daring architectural innovation which, departing from late Gothic principles, clearly heralded the new refinements brought by the Renaissance. Lit by five large antique chandeliers made of tin (16th century), the president of the Republic was elected in this room. From here there is a splendid view over the gardens to the south and, built by Vladislav Jagellonsky for his son Ludvík, the Renaissance south wing (also known as the **Ludvík Wing**) with a splendid panoramic balcony, is reached. Located here are the two **Halls of the Chancellery of Bohemia**, where the supreme institutional body after the sovereign met. The first was the officials' room and has an elegant late Gothic vault decorated with a web of ribbing, while the second is noted for having been the setting for the episode known as the Prague Defenestra-

*View of the Third Courtyard, with the statue of
St George facing the entrance to the Royal Palace.*

tion. Many other rooms in the Royal Palace are worthy of note: the brightly-lit Renaissance **Council Room of the Imperial Court**, where in 1621 the sentence of death by beheading of the nobles who had taken part in the rebellion against the Hapsburgs was publicly announced; the four rooms of the 16th-century **New Land Property Registry** connected to the Vladislav Hall by an attractive spiral stairway; the **Room of the Diet** on the north east of the Vladslav Hall. This is situated in the wing built by Wenceslas IV and restructured by Vladislav Jagellonsky, destroyed by the fire of 1541 and rebuilt by the architect Wohlmut, who chose to replace the ribs so characteristic of Gothic vaults, though purely as a decorative element. Seat of the supreme tribunal and of the assembly of the Czech States, this room is now furnished with 19th century pieces though they reproduce the appearance of some two centuries earlier when, in 1627 the king, seated on the throne and with the archbishop of Prague at his side, promulgated the governmental provisions that drastically reduced the privileges and rights of the rebellious Czech States. Splendidly presented in this room are the *tribune* used by the clerks and the large *portraits* of the principal members of the imperial family – Maria Theresa and her husband, Franz of Lorraine, Joseph II, Leopold II and Francis II. Further north, on the ground floor, at the point of the Equestrian Stair, is the surviving part of the Gothic wing. This formed part of the palace of Charles IV, with the Office of the **Old Land Registry**, probably dating from the time of Oldrich II and damaged by the 1541 fire which also destroyed most of the archives with incalculable losses; the arcaded **courtyard** dating from the time of Charles IV, though some arches were bricked up by his son Wenceslas. Also here are the 14th century **Gothic Hall** under the floor of which an even older Romanesque room has been discovered, and the **Hall of Charles IV**, created by joining together three separate rooms, while Charles' son Wenceslas IV was responsible for the curved vaulting. This room now houses

The majestic Vladislav Hall

interesting models that illustrate the historical and architectural evolution of the old Royal Palace. Lastly is the elegant **Wenceslas IV Hall of Columns**, named for the two columns that support the vault. Following the subsequent phases of building, the older Romanesque complex has now receded to the state and position of underground rooms (and in the course of centuries they have also been used as cellars). However, still surviving beside the remains of some ancient fortifications are interesting traces of the old *south gate* and a large *hall* with barrel vaulting, almost 50 metres long, providing access to the crypt of the neighbouring Chapel of All Saints.

The Hall of the Diet, with the stately royal throne and 19th century furnishings.

The façade of the Basilica of Saint George. Right, the chapel where the remains of Saint Ludmilla are conserved, and below, a view of the nave.

ST GEORGE'S MONASTERY AND BASILICA
Klášter sv. Jiří - Bazilika sv. Jiří

St George's was originally the main square in the Castle and, before the building of the Cathedral, was much larger than today. Prince Vratislav I had a single nave church built here in 920, consecrated in 925 and destined to house the remains of the first Czech martyr, his mother princess Ludmilla, who was canonised shortly after and was also the grandmother of another, future saint, Wenceslas the son of Vratislav. In 973 Boleslaus II and his sister, the abbess Mlada, built the neighbouring monastery and it consequently became necessary to enlarge this little church transforming it into a basilica with three naves, three apses to the east and two crypts. In the years to come the Přemyslid sovereigns were to be buried here, signifying the importance this religious building had now acquired. Seriously damaged during the siege of 1142, the church was rebuilt quite a bit longer, and with two **towers**, the more northerly one of which would be integrated into the cloister during the Baroque period, while the more southerly one was probably built on the spot where the Chapel of the Virgin Mary had stood in the past, probably over the site of the original burial place of St Ludmilla. The **chapel** built to house the remains of the saint dates from the 13th century and is located on the south side of the Romanesque apse (the stone *sepulchre* is instead a 14th century work by Petr Parléř, commissioned by Charles IV). A new *west façade* was made during the 14th century, also by Petr Parléř. It was remodelled with red brickwork in Baroque style in the 17th century and in the same century the **Chapel of St John of Nepomuk** was made in the south west corner of the basilica and decorated with a stupendous Baroque *fresco* in the cupola representing the *Apotheosis of St John of Nepomuk*, by Václav Reiner. The *south façade* is also interesting with a Romanesque wall that encloses a Renaissance doorway leading to the south nave and dated 1515, a magnificent creation by Benedikt

Ried. Originally entrusted to the Benedictine nuns for the education of young daughters of the Bohemian aristocracy, the evolution of the monastery was similar to that of the church. It was also badly damaged during the siege of 1142 but was quickly rebuilt larger and with an additional storey. Helped by the fact that its abbesses usually belonged to aristocratic families, if not indeed the royal family, the convent quickly grew in size and importance, with the addition of a large Gothic cloister, while the abbesses acquired the right and privilege of crowning the queen of Bohemia. Destroyed by the fire of 1541, rebuilt in Renaissance style, completely restructured a century later according to the new dictates of the Baroque style, including an entirely new **cloister** which replaced the older Gothic one altogether, this powerful monastery was suppressed in 1782 by Joseph II and the building was transformed into a barracks. Despite the Baroque façade, the interior of the church still has an austere Romanesque appearance with lofty women's galleries, *funerary monuments* marking the sepulchres of the Přemyslid princes, including the sepulchre of the church's founder, Vratislav I, fine *frescoes* in the conches of the apses and chapels, and a *crypt* with 12th-century cross vaults. Since 1975, on the first floor the monastery has housed the **section of the National Gallery in Prague** dedicated to the Mannerist paintings belonging to the court of Rudolph II as well as Bohemian Baroque works of the 17th and 18th centuries, with works of art by H. Von Aachen, Spranger, A. De Vries, P. Brandl, V. V. Reiner and M. B. Braun.

Adrian de Vries, Bronze horse, *1610.*

NATIONAL GALLERY IN PRAGUE

Jan Kupecký, Portrait of the miniaturist, Karl Bruni, *1709.*

Peter Johannes Brandl,
Apostle, *1725.*

Matyas Bernard Braun, Saint Lutgard by the Cross, *1710.*

Views of the colourful and picturesque cottages in the Golden Lane.

Below, one of the splendid interiors of Lobkowicz Palace.

A panoramic view of Prague from Malá Strana.

GOLDEN LANE
Zlatá ulička

Running in a west to east direction behind St George's Monastery, this picturesque and romantic little street, also known as Alchemists' Lane, is an obligatory port of call for visitors to the Castle and represents the tradition of Prague as a "magical city". In dark and smoky laboratories here Rudolph II's alchemists sought to reveal the myths of the philosopher's stone and the production of gold. The tale is one of the most intriguing to have developed about the city and its Castle. The reality is that the Renaissance houses along this lane were built in the second half of the 16th century to replace twenty or so temporary and ramshackle houses that had sprung up here set against the Castle walls, incorporating the remains of the medieval fortifications to the south and replacing the older defensive terraces to the north, in order to provide lodgings for Rudolph II's servants and guards. It was later that the goldsmiths also moved into this area. Many centuries later, between 1916 and 1917, at number 22

of the Lane, Franz Kafka wrote some of his short stories. Today the little houses that once were craftsmen's' workshops and dwellings for the

poor, are attractive shops where souvenirs and artistic and crafts items can be bought. A quite delightful view can be enjoyed from the castle walls behind, where a long *defensive corridor* winds its way along the top of the houses, still providing a connection between the late Gothic terraces of the fortifications and the Castle itself.

LOBKOWICZ PALACE
Lobkowiczský palác

Opposite the Burgrave's House stands an impressive building structured around two courtyards. The Lobokowicz Palace was the residence of the powerful Pernštejn family during the 16th century and in 1627 after being extended, it passed to the owners for whom it is now named. Between 1651 and 1668 the Lobkowicz family had the buildings entirely restructured by Carlo Lurago in Baroque style. Some of the rooms on the first floor, such as the

two halls and nearby chapel, are still in their original state, while the rest of the palace houses the **section of the National Museum** dedicated to the ancient history of Bohemia.

BLACK TOWER
Černá věž

Closing the Castle and its fortifications on the west are a gate and tower, both interesting remains of what were the Romanesque walls dating from the mid-12th century. The Black Tower was originally known as the Golden Tower after the polished gilding of the roof that glistened at the time of Charles IV, but it was a victim of the 1541 fire which definitively destroyed the gilding and gave rise to its current name. However, the Black Tower was part of the Burgrave's buildings and was for long used as the prison where condemned debtors were held. The Renaissance style *East Door* still has the low Gothic passageway as well as the

pulleys used to raise the drawbridge which crossed the moat in front. Where this moat once was there is now a small panoramic square with access to the *Old Castle Stairway*, leading down towards the city.

The Burgrave's buildings date from the Renaissance.

The sombre Black Tower stands over the eastern gate of Prague Castle

CASTLE GARDENS
Zahrady Pražského hradu

Once the Castle no longer needed to fulfil a function as a purely defensive stronghold, and it had become possible to emphasize its role as a noble residence used for purposes of representation, it was finally possible to develop its more pleasant and enjoyable aspects. Thus, around the perimeter of the fortifications delightful gardens came into being and thrived. It was the Hapsburg sovereign, Ferdinand I, who oversaw their creation in 1534, but their present splendid appearance, enhanced by the presence of numerous Renaissance and Baroque statues, is thanks to the 20th century architect Josip Plečnik who began their reorganization after 1918, an arduous task that is not entirely completed even today.

South Gardens

The **South Gardens** on the southern side of the Castle are quite delightful; they are connected to the Third Courtyard by the *Bull Staircase* and consist of the **Garden on the Ramparts** (*Zahrada Na Valech*) and the **Paradise Garden** (*Rajská zahrada*) which were already well developed in the 16th century, but redesigned and improved during the 20th century by Plečnik. In the shade of the dramatic and majestic south façade of the Castle, skilfully rearranged by Pacassi, the gardens are a series of incredible botanical features, historical ruins and artistic masterpieces. The **Bellevue Pavilion** was made by Plečnik in 1924 with faintly Egyptian overtones and a splendid viewpoint. There is also an **Alpine Flower Garden**, the **Hartig Garden**, which only became part of the South Gardens in 1965, the **Matthias Pavilion**, a cylindrical structure made in 1617 for Emperor Matthias, as well as two little stone monuments close by the Ludvík Wing commemorating the spot where two of the unfortunate victims of the Prague Defenestration fell. Seen from this elegant green paradise, even the Castle seems to assume a sweeter and softer appearance. And from here we return to the Castle, to the west entrance standing at the end of the route through the South Gardens.

Above, a glimpse of the Ludwig Wing, scene of the Defenestration of Prague.

Left, statues flanking the Musical Pavilion in the Hartig Garden.

Below, the Noblewomen's Institute seen from the Garden on the Ramparts (Zahrada Na Valech).

The elegant gardens on the north side of the Castle: above and right, Queen Anne's Summer Palace and the 16th century Singing Fountain. Below, one of the beautiful statues decorating the Real Tennis Pavilion and the cathedral seen from the gardens of the Riding School.

Royal Gardens

Along the fortifications on the north is the crevice of a deep gulley with a stream which, once its obvious use as a defensive feature became superfluous, fell into disuse and was been substantially abandoned, evolving into a pleasant shelter for many animals, including deer. There are no longer any deer, but their presence in the past is still clearly evoked by the name of the **Deer Moat**. The **Powder Bridge** crosses it in the area of the old 17th century **Stables** and **Riding School** as well as the famous **Lions' Court**. At the back of this courtyard lie the splendid **Royal Gardens**, for centuries famous for their tropical plants, the exotic fruits that could be gathered there, and the fertile vegetable gardens. Moreover, it was here that certain bulbs imported from Istanbul were cultivated and the tulips that bloomed were then imported by Holland. It was precisely to provide easier access to this magnificent corner of the gardens that the Powder

Bridge was built in the mid 16th century. The pretty pathways are enhanced by various elegant buildings, such as the large **Real Tennis Pavilion** (the oldest stone building of its kind in Europe, it was built in 1569 by Wohlmut) and the **Orangery**, originally 16th century, but attractively renovated in the 20th century. Also known as the Belvedere for its wonderful view, the **Summer Palace of Queen Anne** is at the end, beyond the small garden; built by Ferdinand I for his wife, Anne Jagellonsky between 1535 and 1563, it has an unusual roof shaped like the keel of a boat and is surrounded by delightful airy arches. It is difficult to imagine that this pretty, delicate building was destined to be used as a barracks and army workshop for almost a century between the 1700s and 1800s.

Hradčany

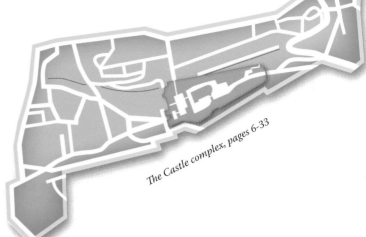

The Castle complex, pages 6-33

HRADČANY SQUARE
Hradčanské náměstí

This charming square, given a certain dignity by the Baroque buildings which overlook it, has always formed the entrance to the Castle. It is adorned with the 18th century *Plague Column* (F. M. Brokoff). The surrounding buildings are the result of reconstruction carried out after the fire of 1541.

The stern statue of Masaryk looks down on Hradčany Square, while street musicians entertain the tourists and passers-by.

The 16th century façade of Martinitz Palace.

MARTINITZ PALACE
Martinický palác

The origins of this Renaissance building date from the late 16th century. During the first half of the 17th century it was acquired by Jaroslav Bořita di Martinitz (the protagonist of the second "defenestration of Prague) who had it enlarged and decorated. Note the Renaissance

34

sgraffito decorations (*Scenes from the Life of Hercules*) on the eastern side. Similar style decorations portraying biblical themes were brought to light on the side facing the square during the restorations done in the early 1970s. It was this restoration project that made it possible to admire the full beauty of the 16th century facade.

The beautiful façade of the Tuscan Palace.

TUSCAN PALACE
Toskánský palác

This monumental, early Baroque style building by J.B. Mathey was erected on the west side of Hradčany square at the end of the 17th century. At that time it was on the opposite side of the castle. It was the property of Count Thun Hohenstein and in 1718 was sold to the grand dukes of Tuscany whose *coat of arms* is still visible on the façade. It is truly a majestic looking building with four wings and two *towers*. The *statues of the Seven Liberal Arts* between the towers on the roof are the work of J. Brokoff. A statue of the *Archangel Michael*, a late 17th century sculpture by Ottavio Mosto adorns a corner of the palace.

ARCHBISHOP'S PALACE
Arcibiskupský palác

The original building was a Renaissance residence which was then transformed in the second half of the 16th century, extended around 1600 and converted to Baroque style in the second half of the 17th century. In the same period the architect J. B. Mathey, who had designed the Baroque transformations, completed the splendid main portal. In the second half of the 18th century J. J. Wirch gave the palace's **façade** its present day Rococo appearance. Above the coat of arms of the Prince-Archbishop A. P. Příchovský is a group of sculpted figures by I. F. Platzer. The exquisite interior furnishings in late-Baroque style are also the work of Wirch. Note in particular the nine Gobelin tapestries, the wood carvings, the stucco decorations and the collections of porcelain and crystal. Ferdinand I bought the palace in 1562 for the Archbishop, recently returned to Prague at the end of the Hussite wars. It is still the Bishop's See today.

Elegant architecture defines the Archbishop's Palace.

SCHWARZENBERG PALACE
Schwarzenberský palác

The sgraffito decorations on the façade of the Schwarzenberg Palace create the illusion of diamond-point rustication.

The building as it is today is in fine Renaissance style, clearly imitating northern Italian prototypes. Its designer, the Italian architect A. Galli, commissioned by the Lobkowicz family, carried out the work between 1545 and 1576. The external decoration, made with the *sgraffito* technique, looks exactly as if the masonry is clad in projecting pyramid shaped stones. The beautiful exterior decoration dates from the 16th century but was renovated between the 19th and 20th centuries. The Museum of Military History collections have been housed in the 16th century wing of the palace since 1945 and are exhibited in rooms of elaborate decoration. They include prehistoric weapons, arms supplied to the various European armies up until 1918, cannons, uniforms, medals, flags, military maps and plans of famous battles.

STERNBERG PALACE - NATIONAL GALLERY IN PRAGUE

Šternberský palác - Národní galerie v Praze

This Baroque palace is named for Franz Josef Sternberg who, in 1976, founded the 'Society of Patriotic Friends of the Arts', to which the members loaned their finest artworks. The collection grew over the years and was transferred to government ownership before World War II. The headquarters of the **National Gallery in Prague** since 1949, the palace has been the home of the **Collection of European Art from the Classical Era to the Baroque** since 2003. The first part of the exhibition is dedicated to Greek and Roman antiquities. The rooms on the first floor house works of art from the 14th-16th centuries from the collection of the Archduke Francesco Ferdinando d'Este, from Konopiště Castle, with paintings by Tuscan masters such as Bernardo Daddi and Lorenzo Monaco, works from the Venetian school (Vivarini's atelier) masterpieces and by the Florentine Mannerists, Bronzino and Alessandro Allori. On the same floor we can also admire the beautiful collection of Flemish paintings that include a triptych by Geertgen tot Sint Jans and a monumental altarpiece by. On the second floor are 16th-18th century masterpieces from the Italian, Spanish, French and Dutch schools by great artists such as Tintoretto, Ribera, Tiepolo, El Greco, Goya, Rubens and Van Dyck. The collection of Dutch and Flemish paintings is dominated by the works of Rembrandt, Hals,

A corner of the Sternberg Palace and the gardens decorated with statuary.

Terbirch, Ruydsale and Van Goyen. The ground floor features 16th-18th century German and Austrian paintings by artists such as Lucas Cranach and Hans Baldung, but the highlight is Albrecht Dürer's masterpiece, *The Feast of the Rose Garlands* (1506), that was brought to Prague by Rudolph II.

A collection of small sculptures, drawings and prints completes the exhibition.

NATIONAL GALLERY IN PRAGUE

Jan Brueghel The Elder, Bouquet of Flowers, *17th century.*

Lucas Cranach the Elder, Adam and Eve, *ca.1538*

Agnolo Bronzino, Eleonora di Toledo, *1543*

Domenikos Theotokopoulos, "El Greco", Praying Christ, *1595*

CZERNIN PALACE
Černínský palác

Now the seat of the Ministry of Foreign Affairs, the distinguishing marks of this majestic building are its imposing size and the massive colonnade which runs the length of the façade. The exterior of the ground floor is constructed with massive diamond-pointed rustication. Work was begun on the palace in the second half of the 17th century by order of the Ambassador to Venice, Count Czernin of Chudenice. It was completed towards the end of the century under the supervision of his son, Hermann Czernin. The many eminent Italian artists, including F. Caratti, who took part in the construction of the palace made some outstanding contributions. In the first half of the 18th century the adjoining **garden** was added, as was the magnificent stairway with its ceiling fresco by V. V. Reiner (*Fall of the Titans*). During the same period, F. M. Kaňka made some adjustments to the building. Towards the middle of the 18th century, following the French occupation, renovation work was required, and this was carried out by A. Lurago who added three doorways and rebuilt the garden *Orangery* in Rococo style. Around this time I. F. Platzer produced several sculptures which now decorate the palace halls. In 1948 Jan Masaryk, son of Tomáš Garrigue Masaryk the first Czech president, died here in obscure circumstances that remain a mystery.

Above, a detail of the mighty colonnade on the Czernin Palace

The famous 'U černého vola' (The Black Ox) brewery and the old Hradčany town hall, two fine buildings on Loretánská, a picturesque street that leads to Hradčany Square.

THE LORETO
Loreta

The origins of this sanctuary, which ranks as one of the most visited religious destinations and places of pilgrimage in the whole of Bohemia, date back to the 18th century, although the legend which tells of the transportation of the Santa Casa from Nazareth to Loreto is much older (13th century). Following the Counter-Reformation, a great number of sanctuaries modelled on the one in Loreto were built in order to promote Catholicism in previously Protestant areas. The **façade** of the sanctuary was begun after 1721 by the Dientzenhofers, who had been commissioned by the Prince of Lobkowicz and his wife Eleanor Caroline. The main entrance is distinguished by the statues of *Saints* and the marble coats of arms which stand above it, all by F. Kohl. The Baroque bell tower houses a set of 27 bells (1694) which ring out in honour of the Virgin every hour.

A detail of the bell tower.

Santa Casa Chapel

This chapel was completed in the first half of the 17th century by G. B. Orsi from Como. It is located in the Cloisters, surrounded by porticoes and decorated with two fountains. The external decorations are either inspired by *Episodes from the Life of the Virgin Mary*, the *Legend of the Santa Casa*, while others represent *Prophets from the Old Testament* and *Pagan Sibyls*. The **interior** of the chapel, which was beautifully painted by the 17th century artist from Malá Strana, F. Kunz, contains an ornate silver altar, a wooden *Madonna*, and various silver decorations weighing a total of over 50 kg. The atmosphere inside is tranquil and enchanting; a splendid iconostasis stands before the image of the Virgin Mary. On either side of the Santa Casa are two 18th century *fountains* representing the *Assumption* and the *Resurrection*.

Left, the entrance to the Loreto Sanctuary on Loretánksé Square.

A detail of the cloister facing the Chapel of the Holy House – or Santa Casa - with the bell tower and the Fountain of the Assumption.

TREASURY

It is also worth visiting the interesting *Treasury*, situated in the upper passage of the cloister. It contains liturgical items, chasubles and some valuable 16th-18th century monstrances, including several exquisite examples, decorated with pearls, diamonds and other precious stones. Some of these priceless jewels were made in Vienna by J. Künischbauer and M. Stegner, jewellers to the Habsburg Court. One of the most famous is the *Prague Sun*, a monstrance decorated with 6222 diamonds.

Just a few of the magnificent items in the Treasury: the Sun of Prague (right) and the magnificent Lobkowicz chalice dating from the first half of the 17th century (centre).

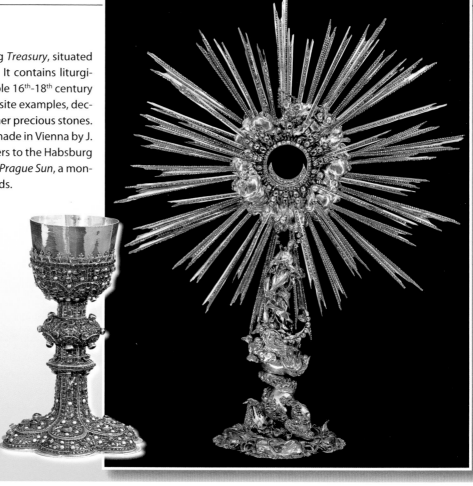

Cloister

The structure dates from the first half of the 17th century and is adorned with 18th century frescoes by F. A. Scheffler. The chapels surrounding the cloister are richly decorated with frescoes, paintings and sculptures, and contain wooden confessionals and altar frontals of excellent craftsmanship.

Left, a view of the Chapel of Our Lady of Sorrows showing the frescoed dome and altar-frontal.

Below, the interior of the Chapel of the Santa Casa with the altar in the foreground.

Two images of the richly frescoed cloister.

Church of the Nativity

The construction of the Church of the Nativity, situated on the eastern side of the Loreto, halfway along the cloister, was begun by the Dientzenhofer father and son team in 1717, and completed by G. Aichbauer in 1735. The **interior** is a genuine triumph of Baroque, with its incredible wealth of decorations including sculptures, wooden inlay work, gold-leafed stuccowork, painted ceiling, angels and *putti*, and multi-coloured marble.

The high altar is adorned with an altar-piece by J. G. Heintsch (*Nativity*), and the vaults are decorated with numerous frescoes including *Christ in the Temple* (V. V. Reiner, 18th century), and the *Adoration of the shepherds*, *Adoration of the Magi* (J. A. Schöpf, 18th century).

The lavishly decorated Baroque interior of the Church of the Nativity. Heintsch's painting of the Nativity above the altar is visible in the background.

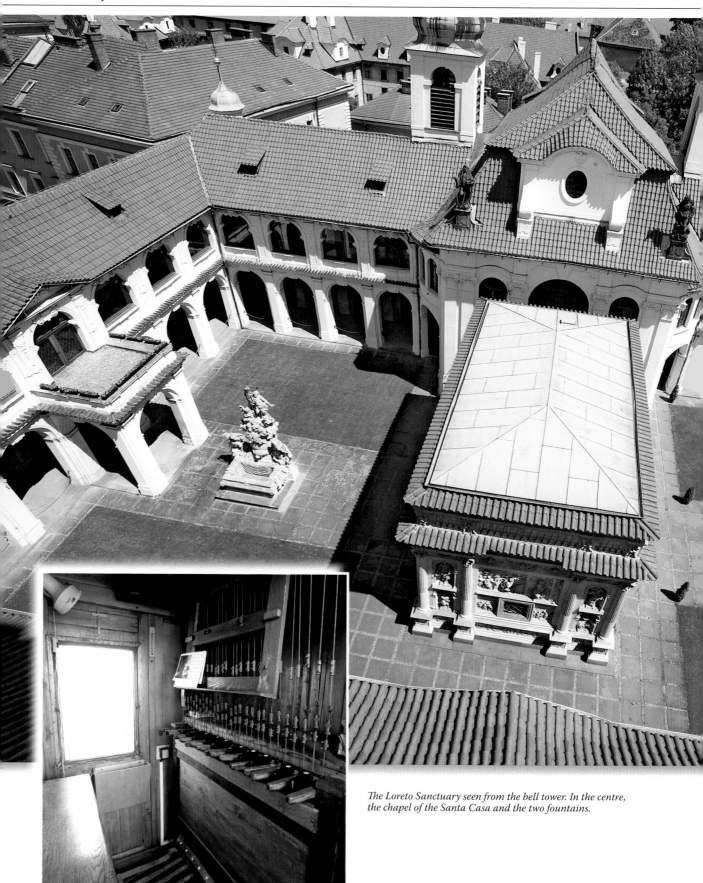

The Loreto Sanctuary seen from the bell tower. In the centre, the chapel of the Santa Casa and the two fountains.

Left, a detail of the bell tower's interior with the keyboard that sounds the bells.

From inside the bell tower, an interesting view with the Cathedral of St Vitus in the background.

Inside the bell tower, the mechanism that drives the bells which play a concert in honour of the Virgin Mary every hour.

SAINT JOHN OF NEPOMUK

Jan Nepomucký (ca. 1340-1393) was born in Bohemia; he was ordained as a priest and became the preacher to the court of King Wenceslas IV. Recently historians have begun attributing his death to the fact that he opposed the royal appointment of an abbot, but tradition maintains that King Wenceslas wanted him to reveal what Queen Johanna of Bavaria had told to him in confession. Because he refused to violate the secrets of the confessional John was arrested, tortured to death and thrown into the river from the Charles Bridge (where there is a cross with five stars commemorating the crime). Still according to legend, five stars were seen shining above his lifeless body. Saint John of Nepomuk was canonized in 1729 and is venerated as a patron saint of Bohemia.

NEW WORLD
Nový Svět

Not far from the Loreto complex is the 'New World', which is in fact a district within a district, and certainly one of the most fascinating areas of Hradčany. It

The hasty visitor can miss this narrow alley – a romantic and picturesque spot with Renaissance and Baroque buildings. An important element in many legends of old Prague, the New World is still a most fascinating place.

is the students' and artists' quarter, a kind of 'Latin Quarter' on the banks of the Moldau, in keeping with the stereotype of the 'Paris of the East'. The former home of the astronomer Kepler ('The House at the Golden Griffin') can be seen here, as well as an attractive Baroque vinárna ('At the Golden Pear').

On these buildings we can still see the cannonballs that were fired during an early, perhaps eighteenth century, war.

The 'Jelení příkop' gardens in this district were recently opened to the public. Here a pleasant walk through the greenery will take us, almost as if by magic, right to the Malá Strana district.

The façade of the eighteenth century Church of Saint John Nepomuk.

CHURCH OF SAINT JOHN OF NEPOMUK

Kostel svatého Jana Nepomuckého

This place of worship was built to plans by K.I. Dientzenhofer during the first half of the 18th century for the nearby Ursuline Convent. The tower was modified during the early 19th century. The **interior** has many fine paintings celebrating the saint.

The ceiling frescoes by V.V. Reiner depict the *Apotheosis of His Life* and the *Miracle of Saint John of Nepomuk*. Some of the eighteenth century altarpieces by J. K. Liška and M. Willmann, depict the *Capture of the Saint*.

The Strahov Monastery of and the façade of the Church of Our Lady.

STRAHOV MONASTERY
Strahovský klášter

This building, founded by the Premonstratensians, dates from the 12th century when it was built under the patronage of Duke Vladislav II and the Bishop of Olomouc. In 1258 it was destroyed by fire and rebuilt in Gothic style. In the second half of the 14th century, Charles IV had the building included within the walls of Prague. It was considerably extended and embellished during the Renaissance, but destroyed by the Swedes at the end of the Thirty Years' War. The architect J. B. Mathey remodelled the monastery complex in Baroque style in the second half of the 17th century. Damaged once again by the events of war (1741), it returned to its former splendour in the neo-Classical period. In the ear-

ly 1950s restoration brought to light the remains of the Romanesque foundations. In the courtyard there is a Baroque gateway, above which stands the *Statue of St Norbert,* the founder of the Premonstratensians. Rudolph II had the former Chapel of St Roch built in the first half of the 17th century; today it is used for exhibitions. Behind the 17th century *Column of St Norbert* lies the **Church of Our Lady,** also dating from the 17th century. Above the harmonious Baroque **façade** stands a *Lamb,* surrounded by the golden epigraph *Vidi supra Montem Sion Agnum.* The **interior** is divided into three naves and is richly decorated in Baroque style; it contains some fine furnishings (scrolls in stuccowork with images of the Virgin Mary). Next to the church is the part of the monastery which houses the **Museum of National Literature** (*Památník národního písemnictví*). The monastery's Historical Library, now once again in the possession of the monks (1992), contains 130,000 volumes, 5000 manuscripts, 2500 incunabula and a large quantity of antique maps. It also houses examples of Czech literature from the 9th to the 18th centuries.

The richly decorated Baroque interior of the Church of Our Lady.

The Library's **Theological Hall** is of particular interest for its fine stuccowork and its 18th century paintings. The barrel vaulting, clearly Baroque in style, is the work of G. D. Orsi of Orsini. The cycle of 25 frescoes by S. Nosecký, the Strahov monk, is a masterpiece in itself. The **Philosophical Hall** is of remarkable dimensions, corresponding to the size of the bookcases housed there.

Two views of the Theological Hall with its magnificent frescoes and stuccowork.

Right, an overall view of the ceiling and below, the grandiose Philosophical Hall.

Below, a detail of the ceiling painting in the Philosophical Hall.

The large ceiling fresco was painted in the 18th century by F. A. Maulpertsch. Also on display in the hall is a *Bust of Francis I*, made in marble by F. X. Lederer in the 19th century. The most notable items in the library, those which constitute its wealth, are the valuable *Strahov Gospel Book* (9th-10th century), the *Historia Anglorum*, the *Schelmenberg Bible*, and the *Strahov Herbarium*.

Malá Strana
Little Quarter

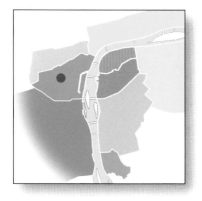

The quarter of Malá Strana grew up, from around 1257, on the left bank of the Vltava, between the hills of Hradčany and Petřín. It was founded by Přemysl Otakar II whose intention it was to create a home for the German colonists. At the time of Charles IV the urban network underwent considerable expansion: old churches were restored or completed, and fortifications and defensive works appeared everywhere. During the 15th and 16th centuries the district was tormented by fires, as a result of which the building and extension work intensified, transforming Malá Strana into a coveted residential quarter. The area was chosen by the nobility and the wealthy for their permanent residences, and they enriched it with sumptuous palaces and magnificent churches. Malá Strana's charm was enhanced by the fact that the coronation processions of the Bohemian sovereigns passed through its streets.

NERUDOVA STREET
Nerudova ulice

This street, which branches off from *Malostranské náměstí* and climbs steeply up to the Castle, is one of the most characteristic and charming corners of the Malá Strana district. One of its main features is its wealth of elegant houses, some of the finest examples of late Baroque building in Prague. Characteristic coats of arms and shop signs, and picturesque front doors capture the visitor's attention: n° 12 was the home of the luthiers, the Edlingers, and the sign with three crossed violins is still here today; **Valkoun House**, at n° 14, was remodelled in late Baroque style by G. Santini; typical signs can also be seen on the houses named **The Golden Cup** (n° 16, Renaissance style), and **St John**

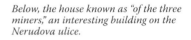

Nepomuk (n° 18, Baroque); the **Theatine Monastery** (n° 24) was the setting for performances of the *Kajetan Dramas* in Czech, while the adjacent building, **The Rocking Donkey**, provided the setting for a story by Neruda; n° 32 is the area's old pharmacy, restored in 1980 and now housing the **Museum of Pharmacy in Countries of the Bohemian Crown;** n° 33 is the **Bretfeld Palace**, also known as *Summer and Winter*; it was here that famous people such as Casanova and Mozart stayed; on the front door of the **House at the Golden Horseshoe** (n° 34) there is an image of *St Wenceslas*; at n° 49 a white swan forms the sign of an elegant Baroque residence. A nearby flight of steps leads to the Castle.

The original decorative details along the Nerudova Ulice: we can recognize some famous insignias such as At the Golden Chalice (top), At the Golden Horseshoe (right) and At the Three Violins (below).

Below, the house known as "of the three miners," an interesting building on the Nerudova ulice.

Little Quarter Square
Malostranské náměstí

The ancient heart of the Malá Strana district centres around two small squares, both surrounded by buildings of considerable architectural importance. The upper square contains the 18th century Plague Column, with sculptures reproducing the *Holy Trinity* and the *Patron Saints of Bohemia* by F. Geiger and J. O. Mayer. Both squares were previously decorated with fountains: the upper one was replaced by the Plague Column, and the lower one by a *Monument to Radetzky* (today kept in the Lapidarium of the National Museum). The most noteworthy buildings are **Kaiserštejn Palace**, created in the first half of the 17th century by joining together pre-existing Gothic houses; the **House at the Sign of the Stone Table** with its prominent Rococo features; **Liechtenstein Palace**, dating from the late 16th century; and the 17th century, late Renaissance **Town Hall of Malá Strana** (the stone plaque on its façade commemorates the promulgation of the *Confessio Bohema* in 1575).

One of the buildings on Malostranské náměstí.

Kolowratský Palace
Kolowratský palác

This late 18th century palace was built by the eminent architect I. Palliardi who designed a magnificent stately home in Renaissance style. It was remodelled in Late Baroque style at the end of the following century and the interiors were radically modified. Two of the rooms are particularly interesting, the **Pink Room** and the **Green Room** as is the original staircase. This building is attached to the **Malý Fürstenberský Palace** (circa 1770) and houses Senate offices.

On Thunovskà street a neo-Renaissance passageway with sgraffito decorations links the two buildings that house the Chamber of Deputies.

A view of the Kolowratský Palace that is part of the complex the Senate of the Czech Republic.

WALLENSTEIN PALACE
Valdštejnský palác

This magnificent residence, somewhere between a palace and a fortress, was built in the first half of the 17th century for the Bohemian commander Albrecht Wenzel Eusebius von Wallenstein. The plans were drawn up by A. Spezza and G. Pironi and the work was carried out by G. B. Marini. The building is a clear example of a residence commissioned by a layman who was antagonistic to royal power. Wallenstein wanted his actions and grandeur to be reflected in the majestic palace which was intended to overshadow the Castle with its size and majesty and this self-congratulatory intention is clear from the paintings which portray him. The ceiling of the **Main Hall** bears a 17th century fresco (*Wallenstein in the Guise of Mars in his Triumphal Chariot*). The other rooms are decorated with paintings, including a *Portrait of Wallenstein on Horseback* in the **Knights' Hall**. The palace chapel's altar is said to be the oldest in the city. The building is also the seat of the Upper House. The **Wallenstein Garden** (*Valdštejnská zahrada*) is also part of the palace complex. It was modelled on the prototype of the Italian Baroque garden, and contains copies of sculptures by A. de Vries. The **Sala Terrena**, with frescoes by B. del Bianco, is used for theatrical and concert performances.

A lovely view of the Wallenstein Garden looking towards Sala Terrena.

Opposite page, bottom the aviary and a view of the magnificent decorations in the Sala Terrena.

The fairytale-like Wallenstein Palace reflected in the pond that graces the stupendous gardens.

The Portrait of Wallenstein on Horseback, by Kristian Kaulfershov (1631) in the Knights' Hall.

The Knights' Hall.

The Plenary Chamber

Left, the Main Hall: on the ceiling we can see the frescoed
portrait of Wallenstein as the god Mars.

Another of the beautiful rooms in the palace: here we can
admire two late 18th century Venetian mirrors.

Commemorative medals are displayed
in the showcases in the Wallenstein Palace
(above and below).

I. třída Řádu bílého lva se stuhou, 1995

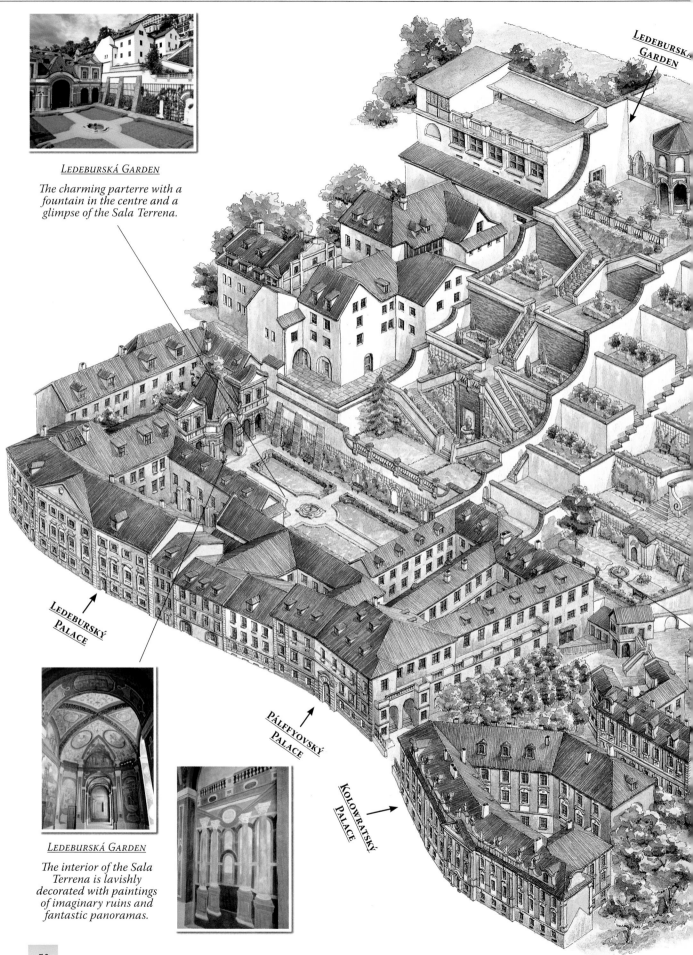

LEDEBURSKÁ GARDEN

The charming parterre with a fountain in the centre and a glimpse of the Sala Terrena.

LEDEBURSKÁ GARDEN

LEDEBURSKÝ PALACE

PÁLFFYOVSKÝ PALACE

KOLOWRATSKÝ PALACE

LEDEBURSKÁ GARDEN

The interior of the Sala Terrena is lavishly decorated with paintings of imaginary ruins and fantastic panoramas.

THE PALACE GARDENS BENEATH THE CASTLE

Palácové zahrady pod Pražským hradem

One of the most recent developments within the area of the gardens that lie to the south of the Castle, below what used to be a powerful system of defensive ramparts, involves the group of gardens collectively known as the **Palácové zahrady**, "Palace Gardens".

In the 16th century pre-existing parklands and vineyards were transformed into splendid Italianate gardens and a century later, following their destruction by the occupying Swedish, the owners of the palaces overlooking the area had a new Baroque layout created, decorated with many statues, balustrades, terraces and fountains. In the late 20th century a sweeping initiative brought about the complete restoration of the old structures and has led to the rebirth of five of the old gardens: *Ledeburská, Malá Pálffyovská, Velká Pálffyovská, Kolowratská,* and *Malá Fürstenberská.* The first two were opened to the public in June 1995, the third in 1997 and the last two in 2000. Admired and supported by the European Union, the initiative has restored one of its most delightful features to the city of Prague.

MALÁ PÁLFFYOVSKÁ GARDEN

VELKÁ PÁLFFYOVSKÁ GARDEN

KOLOWRATSKÁ GARDEN

MALÁ FÜRSTENBERSKÁ GARDEN

MALÝ FÜRSTENBERSKÝ PALACE

MALÁ FÜRSTENBERSKÁ GARDEN

Picturesque view of the roofs of the Malý Fürstenberský Palace.

MALÁ FÜRSTENBERSKÁ GARDEN

This small pavilion is the point where the terrace of the lower garden meets the central staircase. On the ceiling, there is a rococo painting of a swing.

VELKÁ PÁLFFYOVSKÁ GARDEN

A detail of the parterre, in the foreground the ornamental pool with a statue of Triton, and in the background the portal crowned by an antique sundial.

On the following pages the Ledeburská Garden: a beautiful staircase interrupted by Baroque style terraces (designed by I. Palliardi) leads to the parterre at the top of the garden and the octagonal temple. In the background, the Prague Castle.

CHURCH OF St NICHOLAS IN MALÁ STRANA

Chrám svatého Mikuláše

This splendid example of Bohemian Baroque architecture - previously belonging to the Jesuits who made it the focal point of the Counter Reformation in Bohemia - was built on the site of a Gothic church. Work on the building started at the beginning of the 18th century and lasted until 1756 when A. Lurago completed the Bell Tower (79m). The magnificent two-tier Baroque **façade** is decorated with the coats of arms of the Count of Kolovrat and *Statues of the Fathers of the Church* carried out by followers of J. B. Kohl. The chancel and the high dome (79m) are the work of K. I. Dientzenhofer. The **interior** contains some magnificent Baroque ornaments, and the *ceiling* of the central nave was beautifully painted with frescoes by J. L. Kracker (18th century). These show *Episodes from the life of St Nicholas* and are some of the largest of their kind in Europe. The **dome** bears the splendid contemporary fresco (*Apotheosis of St Nicholas and Last Judgement*) by F. X. Palko who is also responsible for the frescoes in the chancel, painted in collaboration with J. Hager. I. Platzer the Elder is the author of the sculp-

The dome of the Church of Saint Nicholas in Malá Strana.

Details of the interior of the Church of Saint Nicholas in Malá Strana. Above the statue of Saint Nicholas by Ignaz Platzer above the main altar.

Top, the grand Baroque organ, and above the richly decorated eighteenth century pulpit.

tures situated in the central nave, the chancel and at the high altar (*St Nicholas*). Also note the 18th century *pulpit* by Richard and Peter Prachner, the grandiose, modern *organ* by T. Schwarz, as well as the altar-pieces and the paintings in the side chapels (works by J. L. Kracker, I. Raab, F. X. Palko, and F. Solimena). Beside the church is the former Baroque style *Jesuit College* which divides the square into two.

A view of the nave reveals the opulent decorations and furnishings.

VRTBA PALACE
Vrtbovský palác

This building was renovated according to the canons of late Renaissance architecture in the first half of the 17th century. The **Garden** of the same name represents a fine example of a Baroque garden and is one of the most important in central Europe. It was designed by F. M. Kaňka, and built in the first half of the 18th century.

Of particular interest are the *statues of Ceres and Bacchus,* of the same period, by M. Braun, the double staircase with Baroque decorations and sculptures inspired by Greek mythology. A beautiful view can be enjoyed from the upper terrace.

A magnificent view of the upper terrace in the Vrtba Garden facing the Vrtba Palace and Malá Strana.

The interior of the Sala Terrena was magnificently frescoed by V.V. Reiner. On the front wall, Susanna and the Elders against a background of ancient ruins; Venus and Adonis decorate the ceiling, and on the sides are statues of Bacchus and Ceres by M.B. Braun.

Below, left, a corner of the garden and the entrance to the aviary; right a view of the lower part of the garden with the Palace in the background; far right, adjacent to the Sala Terrena is the studio of the artist Mikoláš Aleš.

CHURCH OF OUR LADY VICTORIOUS
Kostel Panny Marie Vítězné

The name of the church recalls the victorious Battle of the White Mountain when the Catholic League triumphed over Protestant troops on 8th November 1620. The church, which was completed by the Italian architect G. M. Filippi in the first half of the 17th century, is considered to be the first Baroque church in Prague. It stands in *Karmelitská* street and its **interior** is famous for the much revered *Statue of the Holy Infant of Prague* ('Jezulátko'). This small wax figure (47 cm), situated on the right wall of the church, was brought from Spain as a gift from Princess Polyxena of Lobkowicz in 1628. The 18th century altar bears statues by P. Prachner, and a silver casket of the Holy Infant from the same era. The 18th

The Church of Our Lady Victorious: a view of the exterior and a detail of the 'Jezulátko'- the Holy Infant of Prague, object of devotion for thousands of pilgrims.

century high altar is the work of followers of J. F. Schor. Underneath the church lie the **Catacombs** (closed to the public), with mummified remains of Carmelite friars and their benefactors.

The steps that go from the Charles Bridge to the Kampa Island. Left, a picturesque view of Čertovka and the charming houses that line the street. In the foreground, an old millwheel.

KAMPA ISLAND

This island, mostly given over to parkland, lies between the two bridges, *Most Legií* and *Mánesův most*. The Čertovka (*Devil's Stream*), a branch of the Vltava which flows left from the main course of the river, separates Kampa Island from the picturesque quarter of Malá Strana. During Medieval times the waters of this branch of the Vltava fed several water mills. To

CHURCH OF ST THOMAS
Kostel svatého Tomáše

This Augustinian building preserves clear traces of its early Gothic origins, despite the Baroque restoration work carried out by K. I Dientzenhofer in the first half of the 18th century. The church was founded by Wenceslas II in 1285 as a place of worship for the Augustinians, and was completed a century later. The **façade** is adorned with a Renaissance portal by Campione dei Bossi (17th century), and statues of *St Augustine* and *St Thomas*, a late 17th century work of H. Kohl. The **interior** is remarkable for its magnificent decoration by Bohemian artists who produced a wealth of paintings and sculptures here. The ceiling frescoes (*Episodes from the Life of St Augustine*) were painted by V. V. Reiner in the 18th century and the paintings in the dome and chancel (*The Legend of St Thomas*) are also attributed to him. The 18th century high

The exterior of the Church of Saint Thomas and the beautifully frescoed ceiling over the nave.

altar is by K. Kovář and is embellished with sculptures of *Saints* by I. Müller, J. A. Quittainer, and F. M. Brokoff. 17th century works by Škréta adorn the transept altar (*St Thomas*) and the chancel (*Assumption of the Virgin*). Rudolph's court architect, O. Aostalli, and the sculptor A. de Vries are buried in the church.

The Kampa Museum of Contemporary Art is housed in an old mill.

A detail of the "John Lennon Wall": after the singer was killed this wall was covered with words inspired by him and his songs, and become a symbol of freedom and peace for the young people of Prague. In spite of the regime's opposition, the site survived and is now a popular tourist destination. This image was painted after 1989.

the west the *Karlův Most* rests on the island, and looking south from the bridge along the *Čertovka* the wheel of an old mill can be seen; to the north the stream runs through the charming area known as the 'Venice of Prague', with its characteristic canal and picturesque houses.

travel publications is only partly due to the pleasant nature of its monuments and localities; the term also derives from this iron tower which was built for the Prague Industrial Exhibition in 1891 as an imitation of the Parisian Eiffel Tower. It is 62.5m tall and in the past was used as a television tower. Still used to reach Petřín, a funicular railway was made to transport visitors from the exhibition to the tower. Unlike its French counterpart, the climb to the top had to be made on foot (299 steps), but the view is well worth the effort: on a clear day the 'Golden City', its hills and the surrounding areas are all visible. A lift to the top is now available to carry visitors and the disabled to the top.

MIRROR MAZE
Bludiště

The maze is housed in an attractive pavilion which also contains a wooden model of the Charles Gate, and a diorama of *The Defence of Prague against the Swedes in 1648.* The painting is by A. Liebscher and V. Bartoněk (late 19th century). The Mirror Maze was built at the same time as the Observation Tower and is one of the attractions of Petřín Hill.

The Petřín Tower soars over the eponymous hill, below the cable railway and the Church of Saint Lawrence seen from the tower.

PETŘÍN OBSERVATION TOWER
Petřínská rozhledna

The fact that Prague is often defined as the 'Paris of the East' by

OBSERVATORY
Hvězdárna

The observatory houses the **Czech Academy of Science Astronomical Institute**. Part of the building was opened to the public for the first time in 1928. Guided tours and astronomical events are organised for those interested in this subject. The collection of telescopes used for observations ranges from modern instruments to models now obsolete.

CHURCH OF ST LAWRENCE
Kostel svatého Vavřince

The present Baroque appearance of this place of worship dates back to the 18th century when an earlier Romanesque building, first recorded in the mid-12th century, was reconstructed by I. Palliardi. The **façade** is enhanced with a 19th century *Statue of St Adalbert*, the work of F. Dvořáček. Inside the church note the late 17th century painting above the high altar showing *The Torment of St Adalbert*, by J. C. Monnos. The Sacristy ceiling is decorated with an 18th century fresco illustrating *The Legend of the Foundation of the Church of St Adalbert*.

MONUMENT TO THE VICTIMS OF COMMUNISM

This monument was made by the Czech sculptor Olbram Zoubek to commemorate the victims of communisms. Unveiled on 22 May 2002 at Petřín, it consists of a series of bronze figures, representing the prisoners of the communist era, descending a staircase.

MONUMENT TO THE VICTIMS OF THE RESISTANCE

This 7 metre high bronze by Vladimir Preclick and Ivan Ruller was unveiled on 25 May 2006 at Na Klárové (in the park near the Mánesův Bridge). It depicts a torn Czechoslovak flag, symbolizing the country's resistance to Nazism during World War II.

The Hanau Pavilion in the Letná Park offers a magnificent view of the city.

Letenské Sady

The green hill of Letná (that is, the "summer hill") slopes gently down to the banks of the Vltava and offers a magnificent view of the city, from the Castle to the Cathedral to the Petřín hill. In the area are also the **Hanau Pavilion**, built for the 1891 Exposition and later transformed into a panoramic restaurant; **Praha Expo 58**, the Czechoslovak pavilion at the 1958 Fair in Brussels which was moved to the hill and converted into a restaurant and the **Sparta Praha Stadium** that was enlarged (in the late 1960s), with 40,000 seats as well as well other sports facilities and equipment.

Smíchov

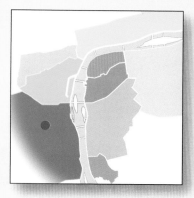

VILLA BERTRAMKA
Bertramka

The villa dates from the 17th century and has had various owners. In the second half of the 18th century it belonged to the Dušeks, with whom W. A. Mozart often stayed, composing and attending some of the debut performances of his works. This Prague residence of Mozart is situated at the foot of a wooded hill with a magnificent park behind it.

The 17th century Villa Bertramka, home of the Mozart Museum, conserves a small collection of Mozart mementoes, along with the Austrian composer's study and bedroom.

MOZART MUSEUM

Named after the great Salzburg composer, the museum was founded around the middle of the 19th century by the Popelkas, father and son. It is located on the first floor of the Villa Bertramka and was opened in 1956. Along with the Smetana and Dvořák museums, it forms the *National Museum's Independent Section of Musicology*.

Note the *Bust of Mozart* by T. Seidan set in the villa's gardens. Of particular interest, besides the composer's study and bedroom, are some of the music scores, letters and historic concert posters. Concerts are held in the villa.

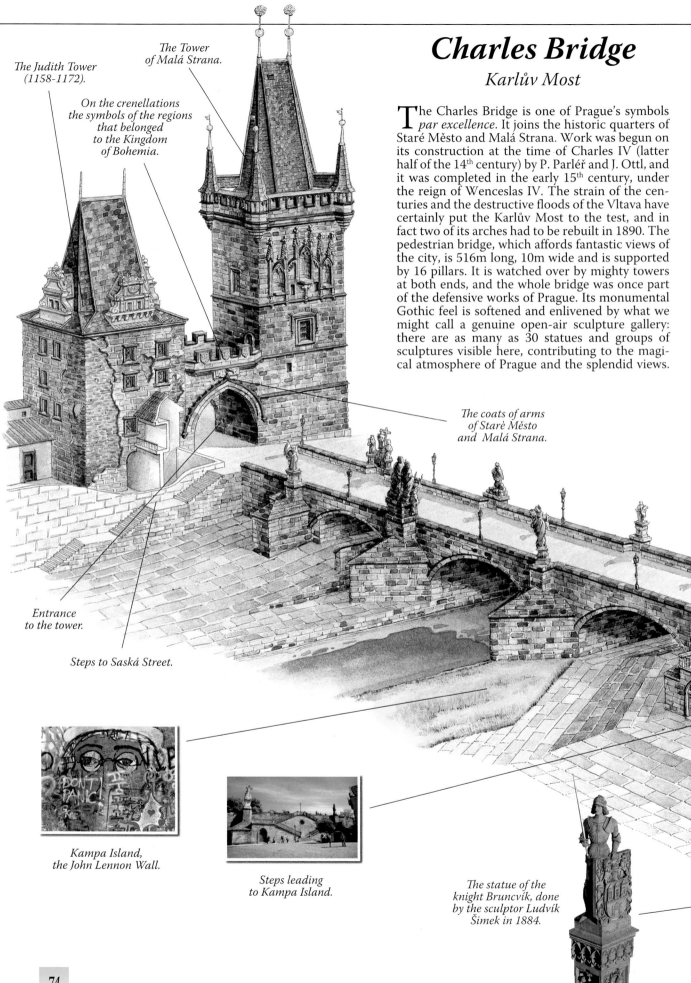

Charles Bridge

Karlův Most

The Judith Tower
(1158-1172).

The Tower
of Malá Strana.

On the crenellations
the symbols of the regions
that belonged
to the Kingdom
of Bohemia.

The Charles Bridge is one of Prague's symbols *par excellence*. It joins the historic quarters of Staré Město and Malá Strana. Work was begun on its construction at the time of Charles IV (latter half of the 14th century) by P. Parléř and J. Ottl, and it was completed in the early 15th century, under the reign of Wenceslas IV. The strain of the centuries and the destructive floods of the Vltava have certainly put the Karlův Most to the test, and in fact two of its arches had to be rebuilt in 1890. The pedestrian bridge, which affords fantastic views of the city, is 516m long, 10m wide and is supported by 16 pillars. It is watched over by mighty towers at both ends, and the whole bridge was once part of the defensive works of Prague. Its monumental Gothic feel is softened and enlivened by what we might call a genuine open-air sculpture gallery: there are as many as 30 statues and groups of sculptures visible here, contributing to the magical atmosphere of Prague and the splendid views.

The coats of arms
of Starè Město
and Malá Strana.

Entrance
to the tower.

Steps to Saská Street.

Kampa Island,
the John Lennon Wall.

Steps leading
to Kampa Island.

The statue of the
knight Bruncvík, done
by the sculptor Ludvík
Šimek in 1884.

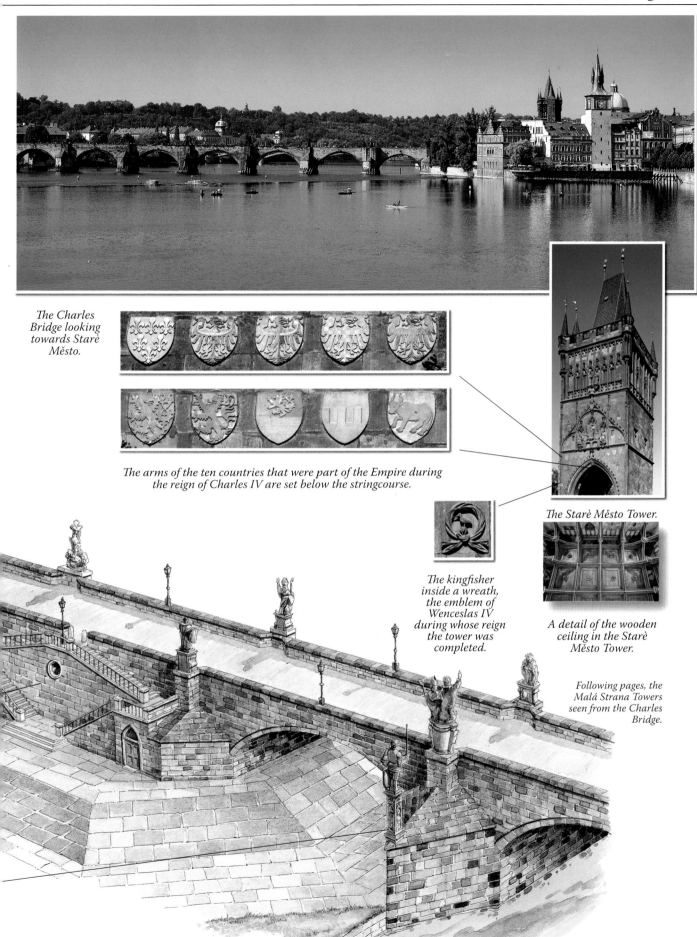

The Charles Bridge looking towards Starè Mèsto.

The arms of the ten countries that were part of the Empire during the reign of Charles IV are set below the stringcourse.

The Starè Mèsto Tower.

The kingfisher inside a wreath, the emblem of Wenceslas IV during whose reign the tower was completed.

A detail of the wooden ceiling in the Starè Mèsto Tower.

Following pages, the Malá Strana Towers seen from the Charles Bridge.

The Statues on the Charles Bridge

1 – Christ between Saints Cosmas and Damian; J. O. Mayer, 1709.
According to tradition Cosmas and Damian were twins of Arabian origin who were doctors in Syria and became martyrs under Diocletian who had them tortured and killed in 287. The cult of the two saints, who are invoked as miracle workers, developed immediately after their deaths.

2 - Saint Wenceslas; J. K. Böhm, 1857.
The patron saint of the Czech Republic and Slovakia in the 10th Century, Wenceslas became duke of Bohemia and worked to Christianize his country. He was killed by his brother in 935 and his remains were later interred in the Cathedral of Saint Vitus in Prague.

3 - Saint Vitus; F. M. Brokoff, 1714.
Saint Vitus is said to have been born to a pagan father in Sicily, imprisoned because of his Christian faith and martyred in 303. He is the patron saint of the dance and is called upon to cure convulsions.

4 - Saints John of Matha, Felix of Valois and Ivan; F. M. Brokofff, 1714.
These three saints founded the Order of the Holy Trinity for the Redemption of Captives, that is Christians who were captured by the Moors. The order was approved by the pope in 1209.

5 - Saint Philip Benizi; M. B. Mandel, 1714.
Philip Benizi was an Italian priest of the Order of the Servants of Mary (Servites). His order began venerating him immediately following his death in 1285.

6 – Saint Adalbert; F. M. Brokoff e M. J. J. Brokoff, 1709.
Adalbert was born around 956 and was bishop of Prague. He was killed trying to convert the Pagans of Prussia to Christianity. He is a patron saint of Bohemia, Poland , Hungary and Prussia.

7 - Saint Cajetan; F. M. Brokoff, 1709.
Cajetan of Thiene was born at Vicenza in 1480. Together with Giovanni Pietro Caraffa, (the future Pope Paul IV) he founded the Theatine Order, with the purpose of restoring the true apostolic life among the clergy. He was canonized by Pope Clement X in 1671.

8 - Saint Lutgard; B. M. Braun, 1710.
Lutgard was a Cistercian nun who lived in what is now Belgium in the 13th century. From an artistic standpoint, this is the most interesting statue on the entire bridge as it depicts the episode in which the saint had a vision of Christ and, even though she was blind, she kissed His wounds.

9 – Saint Augustine; J. B. Kohl, 1708.
Augustine of Hippo (354-430) was a philosopher, bishop and theologian; Doctor and Saint of the Catholic Church. His most famous writings are "The Confessions," and the rule of Augustinian Order I based on his texts.

10 - Saint Nicholas of Tolentino; J. B. Kohl, 1708.
Nicholas was an Augustinian monk. In 1275 he was sent to Tolentino where he preached nearly every day for thirty years until his death.

11 - Saint Jude; J. O. Mayer, 1708.
Saint Jude was one of Christ's Twelve Apostles and according to Eusebius of Cesarea was the groom at the wedding at Cana where Jesus performed His first miracle. After the crucifixion Jude spread the Gospel in Mesopotamia or in Libya; his is the last of the Epistles in New Testament.

12 - Saints Vincent Ferrer and Procopius; F. M. Brokoff, 1712.
Saint Vincent was a Spanish-born Dominican Friar who devoted himself extensively to reconciling the Great Schism. Saint Procopius established the Benedictine Monastery of Sazawa: under his guidance the monks also dedicated themselves to literary and artistic works and expanded relations with the Slavic world. He died in 1053.

13 – Saint Anthony of Padua; J. O. Mayer, 1707.
First an Augustinian at Coimbra, and then a Franciscan, Anthony lived in Portugal and Italy. A professor of theology and a preacher, he fought against the Cathar heresy. He died in Padua in1231 and was canonized the following year.

14 - Saint Francis of Assisi with Two Angels; E. Max, 1855.
The founder of the Franciscan Order was born and died at Assisi (1181-1226). His tomb is a destination for thousands of pilgrims and the city of Assisi has become an international symbol of peace.

15 - Saint John of Nepomuk; J. Brokoff, 1683.
John of Nepomuk is the most beloved saint in Bohemia; he was a priest and preacher at the court of King Wenceslas who had him imprisoned and then executed by throwing him into the river from the Charles Bridge.

16 - Saint Ludmilla; M. B. Braun, 1720.
Ludmilla was the female saint who spread Christianity throughout Bohemia. She was persecuted by Drahomira, who accused her of wanting to steal the throne of the Duchy of Bohemia, and she was strangled to death in 921.

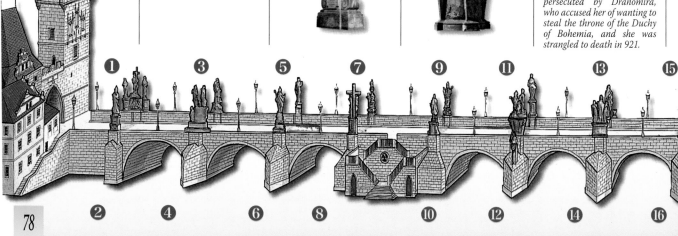

16

17 - Saints Norbert, Wenceslas and Sigismund; J. Max, 1857.

Saint Norbert founded the Premonstratensian Order in 1121. Saint Sigismund was king of the Burgundians. He abandoned Arianism for Catholicism and brought about the conversion of all his subjects.

17

18 - Saint Francis Borgia; F. M. Brokoff, 1710.

Commissary General of the Jesuits, he established the early evangelizing missions in Spanish Latin America. He was known for his humility and great devotion to the Virgin Mary.

18

19 - Saint John the Baptist; J. Max, 1857.

The son of Elisabeth and Zachariah, John is the saint who baptized Jesus and called Him the "Lamb of God." He was ordered beheaded by Herod Antipas because of his preaching.

19

20 - Saint Christopher; E. Max, 1857.

Highly venerated during the Middle Ages, Christopher is one of the "Fourteen Holy Helpers" who is called upon during natural calamities such as plague epidemics..

21 - Saints Cyril and Methodius; K. Dvořák, 1938.

During the 9th century these two brothers evangelized Pannonia and Moravia. They invented the Cyrillic alphabet and translated the Holy Scriptures and liturgical texts from Latin into Slavonic.

21

22 - Saint Francis Xavier; F. M. Brokoff, 1711.

Francis Xavier was one of the founders of the Society of Jesus, the Jesuits, and one of the most significant missionaries of the modern era. He did most of his work in Asia (India, Japan and China).

22

23 – Saint Anne; M. V. Jäckel, 1707.

Saint Anne was the mother of the Virgin Mary; she is the protectress of pregnant women who pray to her for an easy birth, a healthy child and enough milk to be able to nurse the baby.

23

24 - Saint Joseph; J. Max, 1854.

Joseph was the foster-father of Christ and husband of Mary. He fled to Egypt with Mary and Jesus to escape Herod's persecution and returned after the king's death. Joseph probably died prior to the crucifixion of Jesus. He is a protector of the Church and patron saint of Bohemia.

25 - Crucifixion; W. E. Brohn, H. Hillger, E. Max, 17th century.

Statues of the Virgin Mary and Saint John the Evangelist stand on either side of the Cross. The original wooden cross was later replaced by the one we see in bronze; the stone statues were added in the 19th century.

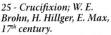

25

26 - Pietà; E. Max, 1859.

In the 19th century criminals sentenced to death were brought to this point on the bridge, they were bound hand and foot and thrown into the river. If they did not die by drowning they were considered innocent and set free.

26

27 – Virgin Mary with Saints Dominic and Thomas; M. V. Jäckel, 1708.

This statue celebrates the bond between the Dominican Order, founded by Saint Dominic and the Virgin Mary. Saint Thomas Aquinas, Doctor of the Church was a scholar, philosopher and theologian and a member of the Dominican Order.

27

28 - Saints Barbara, Margaret and Elizabeth; F. M. Brokoff, 1707.

Saints Barbara and Margaret shared similar destiny : they were both decapitated for their faith. Upon the

28

death of her husband, Louis of Thuringia, Elisabeth joined a Franciscan order and devoted the rest of her life to caring for the sick.

29 – The Virgin Mary and Saint Bernard; M. V. Jäckel, 1709.

French theologian and Doctor of the Church, Saint Bernard founded the Abbey of Clairvaux; he is considered the founder of the Cistercian Order.

29

30 – Saint Ivo; M. B. Braun, 1711.

Born in Brittany in 1253, Ivo studied law and theology in Paris. The saint devoted his entire life to helping the poor and is the patron saint of lawyers.

30

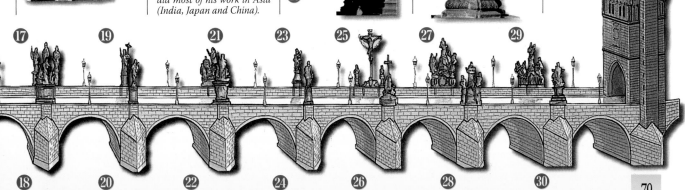

17 **19** **21** **23** **25** **27** **29**

18 **20** **22** **24** **26** **28** **30**

In 1657, following the restoration of a bronze *Crucifix* which had stood here since the 14th century, statues and sculptural groups began to be placed along the parapet of the bridge: 26 of them between 1706 and 1714. Among the artists who have displayed their talents here are J. Brokofff and sons, M. B. Braun, and Josef and Emanuel Max. The group of *St Cyril and St Methodius* was sculpted in 1928 by K. Dvořák. Most of the statues have been replaced with copies since the originals are made of sandstone which is easily damaged by pollution. These are therefore kept in the *Lapidarium of the National Museum*. The *Statue of St Luitgard* is the most valuable, while the figure of *St Philip Benizzi* is the only work in marble. The only bronze statue is that of *St John of Nepomuk*, situated at the centre of the bridge. This is a 17th century work based on models by M. Rauchmüller and J. Brokofff. For luck, passers-by touch the engraved pedestal of the statue representing the saint as he was thrown into the river. On the parapet is a cross with five stars indicating the exact spot from which the saint was tossed to the waters. A Hebrew in-scription near the *Calvary Group* commemorates the sacrilegious act of a Jewish blasphemer (1696) which popular tradition has passed down to us. A scroll situated below the 19th century *Statue of St Francis Seraphicus* bears the verses of Psalm 90/11: "God will put his angels in charge of you to protect you wherever you go". Near the bridge (on Kampa Island) is the *Roland Column*, a 19th century copy of the 16th century original. The bridge is one of the focal points of tourist Prague: it is forever crowded with a babel of visitors, while artists, vendors and craftsmen offer their work for sale in an atmosphere reminiscent of the Parisian *Rive Gauche*. The **Towers of Malá Strana** mark the end of the bridge where it meets the quarter of the same name. The lower of the two towers, from the late 12th century, formed part of the old Judith Bridge. Some architectural and ornamental reconstruction work was carried out on it towards the end of the 16th century. The higher tower, built in the second half of the 15th century, was ordered by Jiří of Poděbrad and took the place of an old Romanesque tower.

The Starè Město Tower from the Charles Bridge at night.

The Charles Bridge from Kampa Island looking towards the Starè Město Tower and the dome of the Church of Saint Francis Seraphicus at the Knights of the Cross.

A spectacular view of the Charles Bridge from the Starè Město Tower with the Malá Strana district and the Castle in the background.

Staré Město
Old Town

KNIGHT OF THE CROSS SQUARE
Křižovnické náměstí

This square opens out from the eastern end of Charles Bridge. It was created in the 16th century and was part of the route followed by the coronation processions of the Bohemian sovereigns. It is distinguished by the *Statue of Charles IV*, cast in iron in the first half of the 19th century.

A view of the Křižovnické náměstí and the statue of Charles IV (1848). Above, a detail.

CHARLES IV

Emperor of the Holy Roman Empire, but also king of the Romans, king of Bohemia, count of Luxembourg and margrave of Brandenburg, this son of John of Luxembourg and Elisabeth of Bohemia was christened Wenceslas on his birth on 14 May 1316 and only took the name Charles at the time of his coronation. The first wife of Charles IV, rigorously of royal blood, was Blanche of Valois, a half sister of Philippe IV of France, who gave him two daughters – Margaret and Catherine. The second was Anne, daughter of Rudolph II of the Palatinate; the third, Anne of Schweidnitz, was the mother of Wenceslas. The fourth was Elizabeth of Pomerania whom he married in 1363 and who was mother to Anne, Sigmund – the future German emperor, king of Bohemia and Hungary, and margrave of Brandenburg – John and Margaret. Certainly a numerous and complicated family, but one that not only supported him when emperor but still accompany him in his eternal and monumental resting place.

The exterior of the baroque Church of Saint Francis Seraphicus at the Knights of the Cross and a detail of the lavishly decorated interior.

From *Křižovnické náměstí*, on one side of the church some steps lead down to the level of the river where the arch of the old Judith Bridge (*Juditin Most*) can still be seen. An attractive little spot for tourists offers boat trips.

CHURCH OF ST FRANCIS SERAPHICUS AT THE KNIGHTS OF THE CROSS
Kostel sv. Františka Serafinského

The plans for this Baroque church were drawn up by J. B. Mathey, and building was completed in the second half of the 17th century. The temple, which was built on the site of an earlier Gothic church, is distinguished by its elegant dome and its **façade**, inspired by French Pre-Classicism. The statues near the entrance (*Madonna* and *St John Nepomuk*) are by M. W. Jäckel. Other sculptures on the façade represent *Angels* and *Patron Saints of Bohemia*. The **interior** is richly decorated, and the dome bears a fresco of the *Last Judgement* by V. V. Reiner (18th century). The nearby *Vintners' Column* bears a *Statue of St Wenceslas* (17th century).

The Baroque façade of the Church of the Holy Saviour, decorated with thirteen statues and five vases, above right, a detail of the façade.

CHURCH OF THE HOLY SAVIOUR
Kostel sv. Salvátora

This church, once part of the *Clementinum* (situated next to the church), is a Jesuit temple, built between the 16th and 17th centuries in Renaissance style. The porch in front of the main portal was added in the 17th century by C. Lurago and F. Caratti; the sculptures and vases which decorate it are the work of J. J. Bendl. The addition of the towers in the 18th century marked the completion of the church's construction. The **interior** boasts a 17th century ceiling fresco (*The Four Quarters of the World*, by K. Kovář).

CLEMENTINUM
Klementinum

Formerly the Jesuit College, this building is considered to be the most impressive architectural complex in the capital, after the Castle. An entire district, including elegant homes, churches and gardens, was demolished in the second half of the 16th century in order to make way for the complex. The reason for this was to support the Jesuit apostolate in their efforts to expand and consolidate Catholicism in Prague. This grandiose scheme of urban reconstruction was planned by F. Caratti and F. M. Kaňka. The 17th century main **façade** is decorated with stucco ornaments and busts of *Roman Emperors*. The **interior** houses the **National Library** (numbering more than six million volumes, 6000 manuscripts, including the valuable *Vyšehrad Codex*, and 4000 incunabula). The *Hall of the Jesuit Library* is decorated with ceiling frescoes (*Biblical themes, Muses*); *the Mozart Hall* and the former *Chapel of Mirrors* are noted for their pictorial decoration; the *Hall of Mathematics* contains a collection of globes and antique table clocks. Also of interest, in the south-western courtyard (not always open), is the *Statue of the Prague Student*, in memory of those who defended the Charles Bridge at the end of the Thirty Years' War.

The Clementinum from the Astronomical Tower.

A section of one of the rooms in the National
Library; the ceiling was splendidly frescoed
by Jan Hiebl in 1727.

Allegory of Mathematics, a detail of the top
of the ceiling.

Saint Francis Xavier, detail
of the lower part of the ceiling.

The interior of the Chapel of Mirrors, completed
by F. M. Kaňka in 1724. The walls are decorated
with fine stuccowork, elegant mirrors and four figures
of saints by V. V. Reiner. The ceiling paintings, probably
by Jan Hiebl, depict scenes from the life of the Virgin Mary.
The chapel was deconsecrated in 1784, it was rededicated
and used for worship for a short time around 1816
and is now an exhibition and concert hall.

Some details of the interior
of the Astronomical Tower,
which, in the past served as
the seat of the Astronomical
Observatory of the
Clementinium. The telescopes
were positioned at the corner
apertures and stood on steel
supports. Today, the top of the
tower can be reached via an
old wooden staircase. Along the
climb there are display cabinets
containing interesting antique
astronomical instruments.
The climb is rewarded by a
beautiful view of the entire city.

Allegory of Language, detail of the top part
of the ceiling.

SMETANA MUSEUM
Muzeum Bedřicha Smetany

The *Smetanovo nábřeží* embankment is named after the 19th century composer B. Smetana; it leads from the National Theatre to a peninsula facing Charles Bridge. Of particular interest, besides the *Monument to Francis I* and the 15th century **Aqueduct Tower of Staré Město**, is the old 19th century **Waterworks** for its architectural design and the *sgraffiti* used to decorate it. The Smetana Museum is housed here, with exhibits regarding the musician. On the quay facing the museum is the *Smetana Monument*, erected in 1984 by J. Malejovský.

Smetanovo nábřeží: the monument to the composer Bedřich Smetana with the Charles Bridge and the Castle in the background.

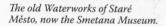

The old Waterworks of Staré Město, now the Smetana Museum.

A portrait of Bedřich Smetana,
composer and dedicated patriot.

The permanent exhibition in the Smetana
Museum that was opened in 1998.

Two rooms in the Smetana Museum
that offers a new concept in museums:
it is place where the visitor can interact
with the surroundings. Each station offers
a piece of music that you can hear in
the room. All you have to do is go to the
raised station and select what you want
to hear. This is certainly a unique
and very interesting way of stimulating
visitors to learn about the composer
and his music.

CHARLES STREET
Karlova ulice

This is a very old street that was on the route of the coronation processions and it still has an unmistakable charm. It is flanked by several beautiful Gothic and Renaissance buildings many of which have been converted into hotels, restaurants and shops where visitors are enraptured by the picturesque atmosphere. The elegant architecture and original decorations are a magnificent backdrop for a delightful walk to discover yet another enchanting corner of Prague.

The House "at the Golden Serpent".

CLAM-GALLAS PALACE
Clam-Gallasův palác

In the southern part of *Mariánské náměstí* stands Clam-Gallas Palace, a splendid example of Baroque art, designed by the Viennese J. B. Fischer von Erlach.
The building now houses the **Prague city archives**. M. Braun and C. Carlone were among those who contributed to the decoration of the palace with sculptures and paintings. Note the 19th century *Vtlava Fountain* by V. Prachner, situated close to the wall of the courtyard.

*Some of the decorations that adorn this very picturesque street.
Left, the original decoration on the House "at the Golden Tiger".*

The Clam-Gallas Palace: a detail of the "Giants" on either side of the portal.

The typical shops along Karlova ulice are housed in elegant buildings.

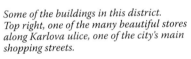

Some of the buildings in this district.
Top right, one of the many beautiful stores
along Karlova ulice, one of the city's main
shopping streets.

The façade of Rott House and a glimpse
of Seminářská Street.

OLD TOWN SQUARE
Staroměstské náměstí

This huge square is the thriving heart of old Prague. Its historical importance, on the right bank of the Vtlava, can be compared to that of the Castle on the opposite side of the river. *Staroměstské náměstí* is not merely an impressive blend of architectural styles and monuments; it represents the very essence of the city itself. It has been the setting for the many events, both happy and tragic, which have marked Prague's long history: in 1422 the preacher J. Želivský was executed here (a plaque commemorates the event); in 1621 the leaders of the Protestant revolt were executed (see commemorative plaque); in 1915 the bronze *Jan Hus Monument* was inaugurated, on the occasion of the 5th centenary of his death (the work is by L. Šaloun, and an epigraph reads *Love and be truthful to each other*); in 1945 the people of Prague joyfully welcomed the Soviet army at the end of the Second World War; in 1968 the crowd bombarded Soviet tanks with Molotov cocktails for shattering the dream of the "Prague Spring", and the Hus Monument was veiled as a sign of mourning. The square at night, with its carefully studied illumination, is especially charming: the lights create surreal, fantastic, almost fairy-tale dimensions on the façades of the noble buildings and up towards the incredible spires of the **Church of Our Lady of Týn**. All around, in the square and along *Karlova*, jugglers and musicians brighten the city's evenings, again offering a typically "Parisian" image.

A magnificent view from the tower of the Staré Město town hall towards Staroměstské náměstí and the city that seems dominated by the spires of the bell towers of the Church of Our Lady of Týn.

OLD TOWN HALL
Staroměstská radnice

The history of this building begins in the 12th century and continues uninterrupted, through various periods of extension, damage, destruction and reconstruction, right up until the last restoration work carried out between 1978 and 1981. The original central part of the building was constructed in 1338; a tower was then added in 1364. **Kříž House** was built before this, in 1360, and is particulary notable for its lively paintwork and the epigraph *Praga caput regni*. Serious damage was inflicted on the complex at the end of the Second World War. The **Council Chamber** has maintained its Gothic character which originates from the

Staré Město Town Hall and its tower seem from the old city square, and a detail of the building.

second half of the 15th century. The huge **Meeting Hall** contains paintings by V. Brožík (*Jiří z Poděbrad elected King of Bohemia, J. Hus before the Council of Constance*). There is a charming view from the top of the 69m high **Old Town Hall Tower**, which can be reached by lift.

ASTRONOMICAL CLOCK
Orloj

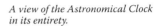

The clock was built by Master Mikuláš of Kadaň and was mounted in the lower part of the Old Town Hall Tower at the beginning of the 15th century.

At the end of the century Master Hanuš of Růže was responsible for its rebuilding, and in the second half of the 16th century it was perfected and enlarged by J. Táborský. Every hour the charming *Procession of Apostles* appears with its eloquent allegories, attracting the surprised attention of tourists and visitors who crowd round in the attractive little square below.

The upper face of the Astronomical Clock showing old Bohemian Time, real time, the visible portion of the sky divided into twelve parts and the paths of the sun and moon through the twelve signs of the zodiac.

A view of the Astronomical Clock in its entirety.

The figures on the sides of the lower face of the Astronomical Clock portray four virtues.

The figures on the sides of the upper face represent vanity, greed, death and lust (bottom).

CHURCH OF OUR LADY OF TÝN

Kostel Panny Marie před Týnem

This mighty construction, one of the capital's most famous symbols, rises high above the rooftops of old Prague. The present day building was erected on the site of an earlier Romanesque church in the second half of the 14th century, and the choir was completed towards the end of that century. The **façade,** in all its austere, Gothic magnificence, was completed in the second half of the 15th century at the request of Jiří of Poděbrady. The tympanum contains a *Statue of the Madonna*, and the façade is dominated by twin *bell towers*, although these were built at different times (the northern one in the 15th century and the southern one in the 16th century). They are both 80m high and crowned with soaring pinnacles and angular turrets which contribute to the fairy-tale setting. The high, majestic **interior** is distinguished by the mighty pillars which separate the three naves and support the imposing ogival arches. The ceiling above the naves is formed of cross-vaults. Fine wooden *altars* with gold-leaf work stand against the pillars. The Church also contains the *Tomb of Tycho Brahe*, Court Astronomer to Rudolph II; a Gothic *Madonna and Child* (15th century); and the late-Gothic canopy by M. Rejsek (late 15th century). The paintings on the high altar (*Holy Trinity and Assumption of the Virgin*) are by Karel Škréta (17th century).

The majestic Church of Our Lady of Týn, with its pointed bell towers dominates the historic centre and spectacular square of Staré Město. A detail of the church façade showing the tympanum and statue of the Virgin Mary.

A breathtaking view of the rooftops of Staré Město from the Town Hall tower.

The Storch House is richly decorated with sgraffito work; a painting of St. Wenceslas on horseback by Mikoláš Aleš adorns the façade.

HOUSE 'AT THE GOLDEN UNICORN'
U Zlatého jednorožce

This building, at n° 20, was extended as early as the 14th century, and towards the end of the following century it was rebuilt in late-Gothic style. The **façade** bears the hallmark of the late Baroque period and dates from the 18th century. A plaque here commemorates the famous composer, B. Smetana, who opened his first music school in this house.

STORCH HOUSE
Štorchův dům

This lovely building, situated at the southern side of the square at n° 16, close to *Celetná ulice*, is distinguished by its beautiful decorations and the architectural details which ennoble the fine **façade**. The painting which adorns the façade, and which recalls the type of fresco-decorated houses common among the aristocratic residences of central Europe, depicts *St Wenceslas on horseback*. Originally a 14th-15th century Gothic residence, Storch House was restored in Neo-Renaissance style towards the end of the 19th century and remains as such today. The building next door, known as the **House 'at the Stone Ram'** (n° 17), is also called *At the Unicorn* after the subject of the bas-relief which decorates the façade.

Top right, a detail of the Kříž House showing the inscription 'Praga caput regni' above an elegant window. Below, some of the historical buildings around the Staré Město square, including the "House of the Minute" that is richly decorated with sgraffito work.

Left, other fine buildings facing onto the Staré Město square: the House at the Golden Unicorn, the House at the Stone Ram and Storch House, the first, fourth and fifth on the right, respectively.

GOLTZ-KINSKÝ PALACE
Palác Goltz-Kinských

This impressive late Baroque palace, which enlivens the eastern side of the square with its Rococo and neo-classical designs, was created when a Romanesque building and an early Gothic house were joined together. Count J. E. Goltz entrusted the project to K. I. Dientzenhofer, while the actual building work was carried out by A. Lurago in the latter half of the 18th century. It was subsequently acquired by Prince R. Kinský. Note the **façade** and its interesting features: the pilasters, the triangular tympanums, the long balcony resting on the columns situated on either side of the portals, the windows decorated with stuccowork and Rococo patterns, and the statues situated on the attic. The palace houses the **Permanent Exhibition of Bohemian Landscape Painting of the National Gallery in Prague**.

HOUSE 'AT THE STONE BELL'
Dům 'U kamenného zvonu'

The building's elegant Gothic **façade** was only rediscovered in the 1960s when some reconstruction work brought it to light underneath a dubious late 19th-century addition. The origins of the house date back to the 13th century, and its name is already mentioned in 15th century records. Its appearance was then gradually altered until no trace remained of the beautiful building which, however, visitors can now appreciate once more.

Above, a view of the square with the facades of Goltz-Kinský palace and the House "at the Stone Bell".

Left, the tympanum of the Goltz-Kinský palace with the bell towers of the Church of Our Lady of Týn in the background.

Below, from the left, a detail of the beautiful Art Nouveau building, headquarters of the offices for local development, the House "at the Stone Bell," and the Gothic portal of the former School of Týn, that leads into the church of the same name.

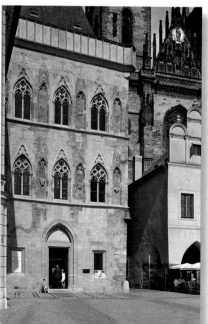

Church of St Nicholas in Staré Město
Kostel svatého Mikuláše

This masterpiece of Baroque architecture was built in the first half of the 18th century by K. I. Dientzenhofer. The monumental south-facing **façade** is a triumph of exquisite Baroque architectural and ornamental patterns. The twin bell towers, the dome and the central part of the façade are of singular elegance. The **interior** consists of a central nave with side **chapels**. The ceiling is decorated with scenes from the *Lives of St Nicholas and St Benedict,* and the frescoes in the side chapels and presbytery are the work of P. Asam the Elder. The *Statue of St Nicholas* on the side façade was added at the beginning of the 20th century and is by B. Šimonovský.

The Church of Saint Nicholas at Staré Město, a masterpiece of Baroque architecture. Above, the elegant dome and a night time view.

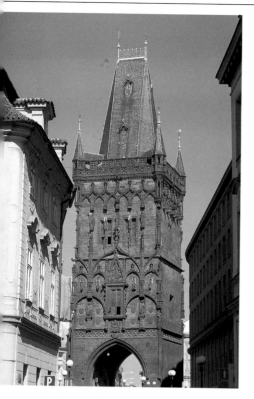

CELETNÁ STREET
Celetná ulice

In the second half of the 1980s this important thoroughfare of Staré Město regained some of its past grandeur. It became and remained an important road in ancient times, and was also on the route followed by the coronation processions of Bohemian sovereigns. Today the *Celetná ulice* is noted for the majestic, Baroque constructions which line the street, the result of remodelling earlier buildings from the Romanesque and Gothic periods. The balustrade at **Sixt House**, situated at n° 2, bears some remarkable sculptures attributed to A. Braun. At n° 12 stands the former **Hrzán Palace** with its attractive façade decorated with sculptures from the F. M. Brokoff workshop; G. B. Aliprandi was probably responsible for the reconstruction of the façade. Note the coat of arms which adorns the door of the building at n° 16. A characteristic *Vinárna* has been opened in **Menhart House** at n° 17. Some of the buildings are now used by the University of Prague (n°s 20-22). The Baroque façade of the house at n° 23 is adorned with an

The Powder Tower, one of the most famous monuments in the Czech capital.

18th century *Statue of the Virgin* by M. B. Braun. Note also the buildings at n° 31 (the Baroque **Pachtovský Palace**) and n° 34, the **House at the Black Madonna,** in Cubist style, whose façade bears the sign of the *Virgin Behind Bars*. The **House at the Mint** (n° 36) is a reminder of the Mint which has stood here since the 16th century.

POWDER TOWER
Prašná brána

From the top of its 65m, this majestic tower dominates the important Staré Město crossroads where *Celetná ulice, Na Příkopě* and *Náměstí Republiky* meet. The late Gothic structure was built in the second half of the 15th century on the site of an earlier fortified gateway dating from the 13th century. It was built by M. Rejsek for Vladislav Jagellonsky, and was modelled on the Staré Město Bridge Tower, forming one of the strongholds of the defence system. The name of the tower derives from a gunpowder store located here in the 18th century. Note the coats of arms which decorate it, together with the statues of *Bohemian Saints and Sovereigns*. Fine views can be had from the top, which is reached by a staircase.

ESTATES THEATRE
Stavovské divadlo

This was the first theatre to be built in the Bohemian capital. It was founded by Count A. von Nostitz-Rieneck who entrusted its design to A. Haffenecker in the latter half of the 18th century. The theatre has changed both name and owner several times: it has now re-adopted the name which was popular from the end of the 18th century onwards, and is a part of the National Theatre. On 29th October 1787 the debut performance of W. A. Mozart's *Don Giovanni* was given here. Between 1813 and 1816 the theatre's orchestra was conducted by Carl Maria von Weber.

The Theatre of the Estates General, a splendid Neoclassical building.

CHURCH OF ST JAMES
Kostel svatého Jakuba

The Baroque appearance of this church is the result of several phases of work carried out between the 17th and 18th centuries on an earlier Gothic building. This in its turn had replaced the original 13th century church, itself destroyed by fire. The **façade** is embellished with fine stuccowork figures by O. Mosto; these represent *St James, St Francis, and St Anthony of Padua*. The temple's remarkable **interior**, divided by pillars, is extraordinarily long (in fact, it is second only to the Cathedral in this respect). It also contains some rich pictorial decoration. The ceiling paintings are by F. Q. Voget (*Scenes from the Life of the Virgin, Glorification of the Holy Trinity*), while the high altar bears the painting of the *Martyrdom of St James* by V. V. Reiner. The Baroque *Tomb of Count Vratislav of Mitrovice* was designed by J. B. Fischer von Erlach and executed by F. M. Brokoff in the 18th century. Adjoining the building is the **Cloister** of an old Minorite monastery.

The Church of Saint James.

and other events. There are also smaller rooms used for meetings and lectures, a café and restaurant, all in full Art Nouveau style. One of the most significant events that took place here was the Declaration of Independence of Czechoslovakia on 28 October 1918.

MUNICIPAL HOUSE
Obecní dům

This most spectacular Art Nouveau building in Prague is also one of the most important historical buildings in the whole country. It was designed by A. Balšánek and O. Polívka and erected between 1905-1911 on the site of what had been a royal residence from the end of the 14th century to 1485 and then abandoned for centuries. The **exterior** is decorated with marvellous stuccos and fine allegorical statues. On the façade, above the main entrance is the splendid *mosaic* by Karel Špillar *Tribute to Prague*. The **interior** of the Municipal House was lavishly decorated by the greatest early 20th century Czech artists, including L. Šaloun, A. Mucha, M. Švabinský, M. Aleš and many others. The monumental **Smetana Room,** a concert hall seating an audience of 2000 is in the middle of the building; this room is also the heart of the Municipal House since it is the venue for many important festivals, concerts

The Municipal House, an outstanding example of the Art Nouveau style, with the splendid mosaic on the facade.

NATIONAL GALLERY IN PRAGUE

Master of Vyšší Brod, Vyšší Brod Cycle, Resurrection, ca. 1345-1350.

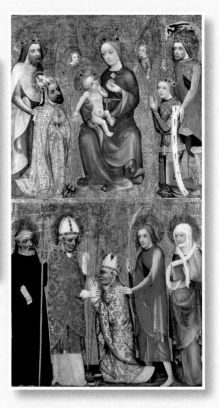

Master of the Altar of Třeboň, Třeboň Altarpiece, The Risen Christ, *after 1380.*

Master of the Michle Madonna, Michle Madonna, ca. 1330.

Votive altarpiece of the archbishop Jan Očko of Vlašim, prior to 1371.

ST AGNES' CONVENT

Anežský klášter

This building, which now houses collections of the **National Gallery in Prague**, ranks among the most important historical constructions in the capital. Its building was requested in the first half of the 13th century by Princess Agnes, sister of King Wenceslas I, whose intention it was to provide a seat for the Poor Clares. She subsequently took her vows in the Order of St Clare and became the first Abbess of the new convent. A crescendo of building activity followed, giving rise to the **Minorite Monastery** (1240); the **Church of St Barbara** (14th century), renewed in Baroque style in the 17th century, the tombs of *King Wenceslas I,* and several Přemyslid sovereigns have been found here; the **Church of St Francis** (mid 13th century) with its Franciscan Monastery; and the **Church of the Holy Saviour** (latter half of the 13th century), an outstanding example of early Bohemian Gothic. It is said to have been the burial place of the Přemyslids.

One of the most interesting collections housed in the rebuilt and restored convent complex concerns **Medieval art in Bohemia and central Europe from 1200 to 1500**.

Saint Agnes's Convent.

RUDOLFINUM - HOUSE OF ARTISTS
Dům umělců

This grandiose construction, with its elegant architectural forms, stands majestically on the banks of the Vltava and overlooks the square named after *Jan Palach*, the martyr of the 'Prague Spring'. It is also known as the *Rudolfinum*, as it was named in honour of Rudolph of Habsburg. It was built in the second half of the 19th century by J. Zítek and J. Schulz. Once the seat of the Czechoslovak Parliament (1919-1939), it is considered to be one of the most outstanding examples of neo-Renaissance architecture in Prague and hosts the annual opening of the Festival of classical music, the *Prague Spring*. An allegory dedicated to Wagner adorns the main entrance, while the balustrade is decorated with statues of illustrious artists and musicians. The **Dvořák Room** is particularly interesting with its fine decorations, dedicated to this famous composer as is the statue in front of the building. Close to the river is the *Statue of Josef Mánes*, by B. Kafka (1951). The nearby *Mánesův most* is also named after this Czech artist.

This graceful winged figure rises on the Náměstí Jana Palacha and is an elegant ornament of the Rudolfinum.

The beautiful Rudolfinum overlooks the vast Náměstí Jana Palacha.

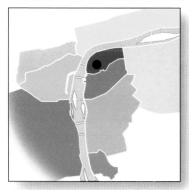

Josefov
Jewish Quarter

Prague's old Jewish Ghetto (*Židovské ghetto*) occupies part of the Staré Město quarter and is important both in terms of its size, and the cultural and tourist interest it provides. The *Josefov* quarter takes its name from the Emperor Joseph II. The first Jewish settlements in Prague appeared around the 10th century, and by the 17th century more than 7000 Jews had made the city their home. Persecutions, fires and plundering were regular occurrences throughout

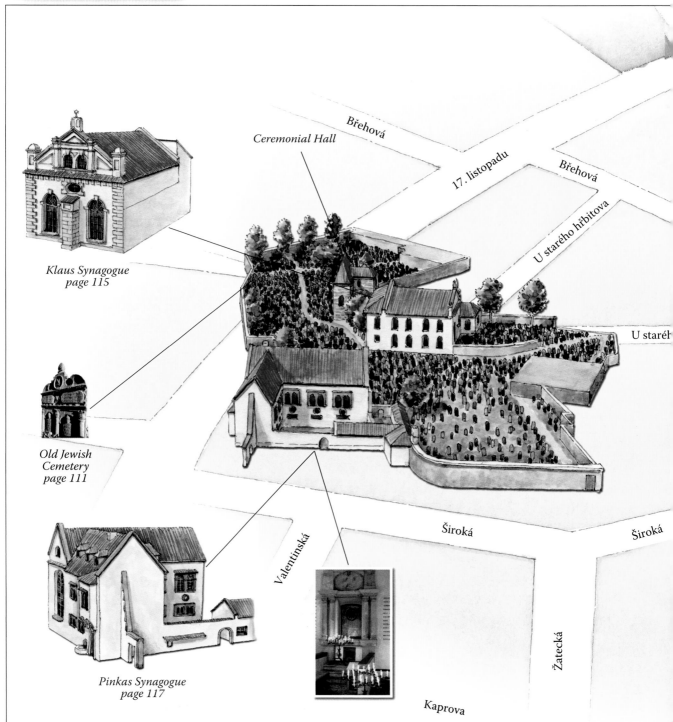

Ceremonial Hall

Klaus Synagogue
page 115

Old Jewish
Cemetery
page 111

Pinkas Synagogue
page 117

Břehová

17. listopadu

Břehová

U starého hřbitova

U staré

Široká

Široká

Valentinská

Žatecká

Kaprova

the centuries, making life difficult for the Jewish community. Towards the middle of the 18th century Maria Theresa of Habsburg decreed that the Jews should be driven out. Later that century, however, the Emperor Joseph II had the walls of the Ghetto demolished, restoring both the Jewish quarter itself, and its administrative status. The area was named Josefov in his honour. Jews were not granted civil rights until 1848. The period of Nazi occupation in Prague (1939-1945) was the darkest time for the Jewish community whose members became the object of persecution and deportation. It is estimated that 90 per cent of Bohemian and Moravian Jews were killed during the Second World War. Used for religious and non-religious purposes, the group of buildings which make up the Ghetto together with the **cemetery**, has now been transformed into a kind of large open-air museum. One of the most beautiful architectural features of the Ghetto is the **Jewish Town Hall** (*Židovská radnice*), a Renaissance building which dates from the second half of the 16th century. It was remodelled in Baroque style in the latter half of the 18th century, and extended at the beginning of the 20th century. Note the unusual clock situated in the tympanum, under the small clock tower: it has Hebrew figures and the hands move counter-clockwise.

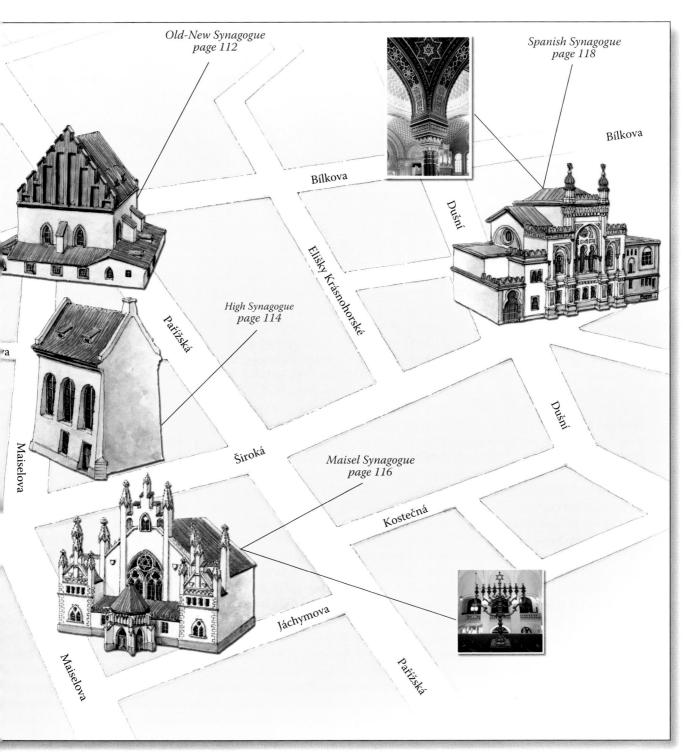

Old-New Synagogue
page 112

Spanish Synagogue
page 118

Bílkova

Bílkova

Dušní

Elišky Krásnohorské

Pařížská

High Synagogue
page 114

Maiselova

Široká

Dušní

Maisel Synagogue
page 116

Kostečná

Jáchymova

Maiselova

Pařížská

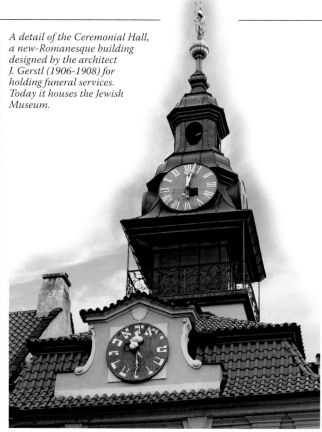

A detail of the Ceremonial Hall, a new-Romanesque building designed by the architect J. Gerstl (1906-1908) for holding funeral services. Today it houses the Jewish Museum.

A detail of the Jewish Town Hall, with its two clocks, one on the tower and one on the tympanum with Hebrew numbers and hands that move counter-clockwise.

JEWISH MUSEUM
Židovské muzeum v Praze

The collections which make up the framework of the museum, and which allow us to understand the development of the city's Jewish community and its culture, originate from various synagogues in Bohemia, Moravia, and Europe in general. Despite the fact that the Nazis wanted to make it into the 'Exotic museum of an extinct race', the number of exhibits increased considerably precisely during the period of the occupation of Prague.

The bronze statue of Frank Kafka, by Jaroslav Róna.

FRANZ KAFKA

Franz Kafka was born in Prague in 1883, son of a middle-class Jewish family. After he earned his law degree he worked for an insurance company and only cultivated his passion for writing during his free time. Although a Czech, his novels and stories were written in German and are among the most outstanding works of 20th century literature (such as *The Trial*, *The Castle* and *The Metamorphosis*). During his lifetime he only published a few stories, the majority of his works were published posthumously. Kafka died in Vienna in 1924 and was buried in the New Jewish Cemetery at Strašnice in Prague.

The bronze plaque in memory of the great writer, outside the house where he was born, at the corner of Maiselova street and Frank Kafka Square.

The tomb of Hendel Bassevi, wife of the first Jew in Prague to be given a noble title (1628).

Starting in the late 16th century, tombstones began to be decorated with symbols evoking the name, family or profession of the deceased. Here we can recognize the blessing hands, symbol of the Cohen family.

The tomb of Rabbi Löw and his wife, is one of the most famous and frequently visited in the entire cemetery (1609).

OLD JEWISH CEMETERY
Starý židovský hřbitov

The feature which makes this site so interesting, and one of the places most visited by tourists, is the incredible number of gravestones it holds (12,000 tombstones, for more than 100,000 people buried here). Because of the lack of available space, they are all packed tightly together, stone upon stone in a picturesque fashion, giving the place a fascinating atmosphere. It is said that in some parts of the cemetery there are at least nine layers of burials. The Hebrew epigraphs and the relief sculpting which decorates the tombstones give an interesting insight into the Jewish community of the time, since, apart from the sex and marital status of the deceased, they also record connections with a particular art, trade or social class of any importance, such as that of a rabbi. The cemetery, which was founded in the first half of the 15th century, continued to be used as such at least until the second half of the 18th century.

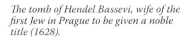

The incredible overlapping tombstones which characterize the Old Jewish Cemetery in Prague.

An interesting view of the Old-New Synagogue, the oldest synagogue in Europe.

The statue of Moses by F. Bílek (1905) stands in the garden of the Old-New Synagogue.

OLD-NEW SYNAGOGUE
Staronová synagoga

This synagogue, originally Gothic in design, was extended in Cistercian Gothic style in the 13th century. Further modifications and additions were completed between the 15th and 18th centuries. Renovation and resto-

Above, a detail of the interior of the Old-New Synagogue with the Aron Hakodesh, *the cabinet in which the Torah scrolls are kept, on the eastern wall of the synagogue.*

A detail of the late-Gothic grate separating the bimah *(the pulpit where the Torah is read) from the surrounding area.*

ration work was also carried out in the 19th-20th centuries. Considered the oldest in Europe, the synagogue is still used for religious services. A *Statue of Moses* by F. Bílek can be seen in the adjoining **park**.

The subdued interior of the High Synagogue with the bimah *in the centre. Today the synagogue is also used by the Jewish Community of Prague for other activities.*

Left, the outside of the High Synagogue, at the top we can see one of the clocks on the Jewish Town Hall.

HIGH SYNAGOGUE
Vysoká synagoga

The High Synagogue was built in the second half of the 16th century, to a design by P. Roder. In the 19th century restoration was carried out to separate it from the **Town Hall**. The central, square hall, originally Renaissance in style, was transformed in the 17th-19th centuries and remodelled in neo-Renaissance style. Note the magnificent stellar vaulting. The rooms of the synagogue are used for exhibitions by the **Jewish Museum** (they contain vestments, manuscripts and precious ornaments). The High Synagogue is closed to the public. Tourists can visit only the ground floor of the building.

KLAUS SYNAGOGUE
Klausova synagoga

The name of this synagogue derives from the term *klausen*, which refers to Jewish prayer houses. In fact the 17th century Klaus Synagogue is built on the site once occupied by the Jewish School of Löw ben Bezalel, a 16th century Rabbi and philosopher. The Baroque building houses a collection of prints and manuscripts.

The Klaus Synagogue seen from the Old Jewish Cemetery with its amazing overlapping tombstones.

The elegant interior of the Klaus Synagogue, with its elegant early Baroque stuccowork on the ceiling, and the Aron Hakodesh *in the background.*

MAISEL SYNAGOGUE
Maiselova synagoga

The synagogue takes its name from the mayor of the Jewish quarter at the time of Rudolph II, Mordechai Maisel, for whom it was originally created as a private chapel. It was built in Renaissance style at the end of the 16th century, and reconstructed in Baroque style about a century later, after a fire. The building as it appears today was restored in neo-Gothic style between the 19th and 20th centuries. The synagogue now houses an exhibition on the *History of the Jews in Bohemia and Moravia from the 10th to 18th centuries*, from the **Jewish Museum**.

A plaque commemorating Mordechai Maisel, the founder, inside the synagogue.

An interesting view of the Maisel Synagogue from the gallery. In the foreground, a fine gilded nine-arm candelabrum.

PINKAS SYNAGOGUE
Pinkasova synagoga

The earliest religious building on the site of today's Pinkas Synagogue, probably a ritual bath (*mikva*), is said to date from the 11th-12th centuries. In the first half of the 16th century a late-Gothic synagogue was constructed in the building which had been the home of Rabbi Pinkas (for whom it is named). This was rebuilt and enlarged in the first half of the 17th century, in late Renaissance style. In the 1950s the synagogue became the seat of the *Memorial of the 77, 297*, a monument erected in memory of the victims of the Holocaust.

A detail of the ceiling in the Pinkas Synagogue with its late-Gothic arches. The grate of the bimah repeats the Star of David motif with the hat in the middle (symbol of the Jewish Community of Prague).

The early Baroque style Aron Hakodesh in the Pinkas Synagogue. On either side are inscriptions with the names of the concentration and extermination camps to which most of the Czech Jews were deported.

SPANISH SYNAGOGUE
Španělská synagoga

The building which today houses the Spanish Synagogue bears some striking Moorish features, added in the second half of the 19th century. The temple interior is strongly

The western façade of the Spanish Synagogue with its rich Moorish decorations.

Below, left the interior of the Spanish Synagogue that is richly decorated with materials and patterns that recalls the Alhambra in Granada. The eastern side is one of the most lavishly decorated parts of the entire building.

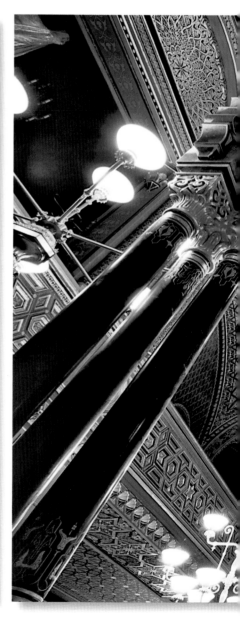

reminiscent of the Alhambra in Granada. The synagogue owes its name to a community of Iberian Jews who came to Prague to escape persecution. Occupying the site of the **Old School**, the oldest synagogue in the city (12th century), it has been destroyed by fire and rebuilt several times.

Right and below, two images of the interior of the Spanish Synagogue clearly show the magnificent decorations on the walls and ceilings. The Star of David is one of the dominant motifs.

Nové Město
New Town

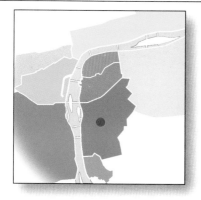

NA PŘÍKOPĚ STREET
Na Příkopě

Situated at the heart of the *Golden Cross*, this street is Prague's lively commercial centre, full of shops, banks, restaurants and office blocks. Its Czech name means 'on the ditch' (in fact, *Na Příkopě* lies along the path of a moat which divided *Staré Město* - the 'Old Town' - from *Nové Město* - the 'New Town'); in the past, before it was filled in, all manner of rubbish was thrown in here and it was therefore actually a ditch filled with sewage. At n° 4 is the 19th century building which houses **Dům elegance**, the oldest department store in the Capital (*Koruna*). At n° 10 is the **Sylva-Taroucca Palace**, a splendid example of Bohemian Baroque architecture. Also worthy of note are the **Casa Slava**, originally Baroque in design (17th-18th centuries) and renovated in neo-Classical style at the end of the 19th century (now a modern shopping centre), and the **State Bank Building** at n° 24, erected in the late 1930s. Previously on this site stood some famous hotels where illustrious figures of the 19th century used to stay.

WENCESLAS SQUARE
Václavské náměstí

The impressive *Wenceslas Square* is situated in the heart of the city. Its dimensions (750 x 60m) make it look more like a Parisian *Boulevard* than a square. It is a lively conglomeration of well-known hotels (like the 'Evropa' at n° 25, a treasure of Art Nouveau architecture), restaurants and cafés, galleries, shops, cinemas and clubs, which together with *Na Příkopě*, *Na Můstku* and *28.října* forms the group of main thoroughfares known as the *Golden Cross*. This is the commercial heart of the Czech metropolis, redeveloped in the 1980s to include wide green spaces, following the building of the underground system. In the square, opposite the **National Museum of Prague**, stands the *St Wenceslas Monument*, the work of J. V. Myslbek (1912-1913). The patron saint of Bohemia is represented on horseback, surrounded by the statues of *St Ludmila*, *St Procopius*, *St Adalbert* and *St Agnes of Prague*. The square was originally founded as a horse market by Charles IV, at the same

The equestrian statue of Saint Wenceslas stands proudly in front of the National Museum of Prague.

Saint Wenceslas Square facing the National Museum of Prague.

time as Nové Město; it was given its present name towards the middle of the 19th century. Wenceslas Square also represents the moral and historical conscience of the newly-formed Czech Republic. In the early months of 1969 it was the scene of dramatic events following the military occupation by troops of the Warsaw Pact (August 1968). On 16th January the Philosophy student Jan Palach burnt himself to death at the foot of the St Wenceslas Monument, and a few weeks later the student Jan Zajíc committed suicide in the same square. Nineteen years later, on 28 October 1988, the Communist police forcefully dispersed a demonstration commemorating the proclamation of the First Republic. Again in 1989 there were further incidents of brutality against demonstrators commemorating the sacrifice of Palach. These events led inevitably to the 'Velvet Revolution' which, within a few months, restored the dignity of a free country to Czechoslovakia.

CHURCH OF OUR LADY
OF THE SNOWS
Kostel Panny Marie Sněžné

This church was built under the patronage of Charles IV, who in 1347 wanted it to be the place of his coronation. Once completed the ambitious projects was to have been even more magnificent than the Cathedral of St Vitus. The 30m high choir had been completed by the end of the century.
The magnificent Gothic portal on the north side is decorated with an abundance of statues of saints. With the coming of the 15th century the church began its gradual decline; the ceiling collapsed during the first half of the 17th and was replaced with another in Renaissance style. This church was also the meeting place of the Hussite movement. One of the outstanding features **inside** the church is the 17th century Baroque high altar, the largest altar of its kind in Prague's churches.

JINDŘIŠSKÁ TOWER
Jindřišská věž

This tower dates from the late Gothic period (1472-1476), after the fire of 1745 it was rebuilt in the Baroque style and then was remodelled, again in Gothic style. The *clock* dates from 1577. The Jindřišská Tower has been open to the public since 2002. It is ten stories high and affords a magnificent view of the city. It has exhibition facilities, shops, a cafeteria and a restaurant where visitors can take a relaxing break.

Top, a detail of the Grand Hotel Europa, one of the finest examples of Art Nouveau architecture in Prague.

Centre, the church of Our Lady of the Snows, an important example of Gothic architecture.

The 66 metre high Jindřišská Tower, offers an opportunity to enjoy an extraordinary view of Prague.

JUBILEE SYNAGOGUE
Jubilejní synagoga

The newest and also largest synagogue in Prague was designed by V. Stiasstný and A. Richter. Built during the early years of the 20th century it combines Art Nouveau influence with pseudo-Moorish ideas. The synagogue was name in honour of Franz Joseph I who celebrated the jubilee (50th anniversary) of his reign in 1898. The synagogue was built outside the old Jewish district and is still used for religious services.

Inside the Jubilee Synagogue, from a side nave, and above, a detail of the beautiful decorations.

The façade of the Jubilee Synagogue, an original blend of different styles, embellished with many decorative and religious elements such as – at the top – the tablets with the Ten Commandments, and the Hebrew verse from Psalm 118:20 'This is the gate of the Lord into which the righteous shall enter." Top, a detail of the exterior that clearly shows Moorish influence.

The impressive interior of the National Museum of Prague and the elegant staircase.

Left, the interior of the Pantheon with a detail of the dome, and below some of the busts of the famous figures in Bohemian history, culture, science and statesmanship.

Bronze bull with iron inlays, from the Hallstatt civilization (6-5th cent. B.C.).

Celtic sculpture (2nd-1st cent. B.C.) from Mšecké Žehrovice (Bohemia).

Late Neolithic ceremonial figurine (latter half of the 5th millennium B.C.).

NATIONAL MUSEUM OF PRAGUE
Národní muzeum v Praze

This imposing neo-Renaissance building, which stands the full width of the southern end of *Václavské náměstí*, was built in the second half of the 19th century to a design by J. Schulz. It houses the main seat of the National Museum in Prague, with the **Museum of History and Natural History**, and the rooms used to house the **Library** (which numbers more than 1.3 million volumes and 8000 manuscripts). The domed **Pantheon** contains various busts and statues representing important figures from Czech culture. The Mineralogy, Botany, and Zoology collections are displayed in the side wings. The Historical and Archaeological sections contain some interesting coins, medals and theatrical exhibits. The National Museum also incorporates sections of the museums dedicated to *Ethnography*, *Musical Instruments*, *Náprstek* and *Physical Culture and Sport*. These are all housed in separate buildings.

Weights, knives with decorated hilts, iron implements, an oil lamp and a whetting stone, from Germanic settlements of the late Roman Era (3rd and 4th cent. A.D.).

A collection of swords and a belt from a tomb a Bučina, gold and silver plated brooches, necklaces and a bone comb from the Germanic civilization from the era of the migrations (5 and 6th cent. A.D.).

The National Theatre seen from the river.

The exhibition space created in the former basement storage rooms of the theatre in the 1980s. Here we can admire 21 stone slabs (and there may well be more) with inscriptions dating back to when the theatre was established.

NATIONAL THEATRE
Národní divadlo

This beautiful building, with its neo-Renaissance architectural features, stands on the right bank of the Vltava. It was erected in the second half of the 19th century to a design by J. Zítek. A short time after the staging of the very first performance the theatre was destroyed by fire and rebuilt in record time by J. Schulz, a follower of Zítek. Careful restoration work was carried out between 1976 and 1983. The modern complex called the New Stage was added in 1983; this also includes the **Laterna Magica Theatre**. The northern **façade** is adorned with *Statues of Záboj and Lumír*, the work of artists from the workshop of A. Wagner. Two groups of statues adorn the attic storey, *Apollo and the Muses*, and *Goddesses of Victory*, both by B. Schnirch. *Allegories of Opera and Drama* attributed to J. V. Myslbek stand above the side entrance, and the same artist also created the busts of il-

lustrious figures. The **interior** of the National Theatre is richly decorated with paintings. The ceiling of the auditorium bears eight *Allegories representing the Arts* by F. Ženíšek who also painted the *Golden Age, Decline and Revival of Art,* which decorates the lobby on the first balcony.

The interior of the National Theatre; the ceiling is decorated with allegories of the arts.

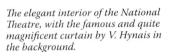

The foyer of the first tier.

The elegant interior of the National Theatre, with the famous and quite magnificent curtain by V. Hynais in the background.

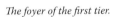

Beer Museum

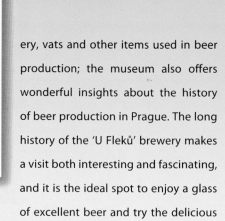

The famous 'U Fleků' brewery still makes beer according to the traditional methods and is one of the most famous not only in Prague, but also the Czech Republic. It has hosted many famous and loyal guests, including artists, painters, writers, and patriots and even occasional visitors who have all contributed to creating its truly unique atmosphere. After its five hundredth anniversary in 1999 an interesting museum was established with exhibits showcasing machinery, vats and other items used in beer production; the museum also offers wonderful insights about the history of beer production in Prague. The long history of the 'U Fleků' brewery makes a visit both interesting and fascinating, and it is the ideal spot to enjoy a glass of excellent beer and try the delicious Bohemian specialties served in the restaurant.

The charming patio of the 'U Fleků' Restaurant.

This interesting museum showcases some of the equipment used in beer-making. Below, two brewing vats.

Below, one of the most interesting sections of the museum with the equipment used for drying malt with wood smoke.

The north side of **Charles Square**, the city's biggest square that dates from the times of Nové Město, when it was the site of a livestock market. It was transformed into a park in the mid-nineteenth century. Beyond the square is the Nové Město Town Hall, theatre of the defenestration of 1419.

The fourteenth century **Church of Saint Mary and Charlemagne** built by Charles IV. The octagonal plan recalls the Chapel where Charlemagne is buried at Aachen.

The marble statue of the writer Eliška Krásnohorská, (1847-1926), by Karla Vobišová. This is just one of the monuments dedicated to illustrious figures from Bohemian history that we can see in the square.

Top left, the **Church of Saint Mary and the Slavonic Patrons** of the **Na Slovanech Monastery** *(also known as Emmaus). It was established in 1347 by Charles IV for the Slavonic rite Benedictines, was an important cultural and artistic centre until the outbreak of the Hussite wars.. It changed hands several times over the centuries and its appearance was also modified; razed to the ground during World War II it was rebuilt with interested reinforced concrete spires.*

Above, right, the Orthodox **Church of the Annunciation**, with its Gothic tower. The vault over the nave is supported by a single central column.

The **Church of Saint John on the Rock**, is a small baroque building by K. I. Dientzenhofer. On the main altar is a wooden version of the statue of Saint John of Nepomuk that stands on the Charles Bridge.

Dvořák Museum - Villa America
Letohrádek Amerika

Housed in the splendid setting of the Villa America, the Dvořák Museum contains music scores, documents and correspondence belonging to the Czech composer Antonín Dvořák (1814-1904) and constitutes a section of the **National Museum of Prague**, (Music Section). It is easy to see why the building is considered a treasure of Prague Baroque architecture. It was designed

A portrait of the composer.

by K. I. Dientzenhofer for Count Michna who made it his magnificent summer residence. The villa, which dates from the first half of the 18th century, is also known as *Villa Michna* and is distinguished by a fine Baroque entrance-gate (a copy), 18th century frescoes by J. F. Schor, and statues of the same era situated in the garden, from the A. Braun workshop.

A view of Villa America, a baroque jewel and home of the Dvořák Museum.

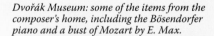
Dvořák Museum: the upstairs room.

Dvořák Museum: some of the items from the composer's home, including the Bösendorfer piano and a bust of Mozart by E. Max.

The "Dancing House" built between 1994 and 1996, is one of the symbols of the new Prague. Designed by the architects Frank O. Gehry and V. Milunič, it was inspired by the famous dancer, Fred Astaire and Ginger Rogers. Also known as "Ginger e Fred", it is an office building.

Vyšehrad

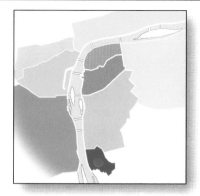

"Vyšehrad" means a 'castle on the heights', and the hill where it is situated is said to have been the seat of the first Přemyslid princes.

It was almost certainly founded in the 10th century as a rival to Hradčany Castle. From the 11th century onwards it became more and more important as sovereigns established themselves here, and the building was expanded. It went into a period of decline around the mid-12th century, and was fortified two centuries later.

The settlement suffered greatly during The Hussite Wars (15th century). By the beginning of the 17th century the area had taken on the appearance of a Baroque fortress. After its destruction in 1911, Vyšehrad is today undergoing careful restoration work.

An interesting view of Vyšehrad from the Moldau.

The Leopold Gate, designed by C. Lurago, is part of the seventeenth century fortifications of the Vyšehrad castle.

The Rotonda of Saint Martin is considered the earliest example of Romanesque architecture in Prague (11th cent. Rebuilt in the 19th cent.).

A picturesque view of the Church of Saints Peter and Paul from the Vyšehrad gardens.

Three of the four sculptural groups which embellish the Vyšehrad gardens: left, the statue of Záboj and Slavoj, centre Ctirad and Šárka, and on the right Přemysl and Libuše.

VYŠEHRAD PARK
Vyšehradské sady

Part of the old stronghold of Vyšehrad is now a lovely park where we can stop and enjoy a magnificent view of the city. On the south side of the **Church of Saints Peter and Paul** amidst the greenery are four groups of sculptures by J. V. Myslbek, inspired by important figures in early Czech history. Originally these statues were on the **Palacký Bridge.** They were damaged during World War II, removed for restorations and placed here in the park in 1948.

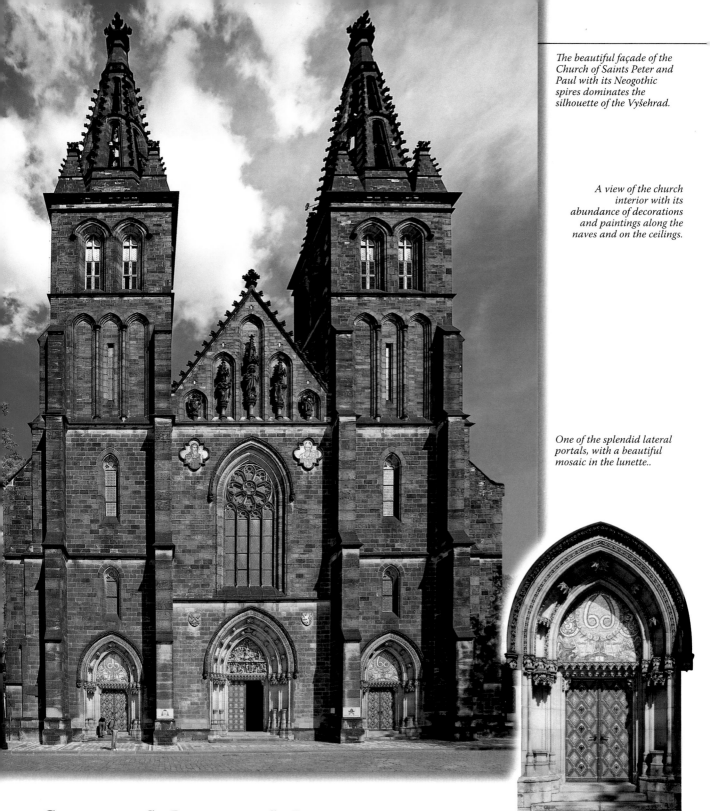

The beautiful façade of the Church of Saints Peter and Paul with its Neogothic spires dominates the silhouette of the Vyšehrad.

A view of the church interior with its abundance of decorations and paintings along the naves and on the ceilings.

One of the splendid lateral portals, with a beautiful mosaic in the lunette..

CHURCH OF ST PETER AND ST PAUL

Kostel svatého Petra a Pavla

This church, situated on the heights of Vyšehrad, is a striking feature on Prague's skyline. Its twin spires dominate the houses which overlook the right bank of the Vltava, built by the Cubist architect, J. Chochol, making it one of the symbols of this quarter of the capital. The first place of worship on this site was built in the latter half of the 11th century. During the reign of Charles IV the church was rebuilt to become a three-nave basilica in distinctly Gothic style. It was subsequently remodelled in Renaissance style in the 16th century, and again in Baroque style in the 18th century. However, the church today offers the neo-Gothic appearance it assumed in the latter half of the 19th century. Further restoration work was carried out between 1981 and 1987, at the same time as some archaeological excavations. The **façade** of the church is wedged between two soaring spires, erected in

the early 20th century and jointly designed by J. Mocker and F. Mikš. The neo-Gothic appearance of the façade is reinforced by its triangular tympanum decorated with sculptures. The lunettes of the magnificent, deeply splayed portals are decorated with mosaics (side portals), and with high relief sculpting (central portal). Note the doors themselves, enriched with coats of arms and precious gold-leaf work. The **interior** contains some nota-

ble frescoes with stylised motives, dating from the early 1900s. The church's charm is enhanced by the beauty of the decorations and paintings which completely cover the naves and the ceiling (which is formed of ribbed cross-vaulting). Pillars supporting ogival arches separate the three naves. Above the side altars, enriched with various works in wood (altar frontals, sculptures, triptychs), there are some finely illustrated windows. The high altar,

by J. Mocker, is decorated with four statues by F. Hrubeš (late 19th century); these represent *St Peter and St Paul, St Cyril and St Methodius.* Note also, in the first chapel on the right, the *Tomb of St Longinus,* an 11th century Romanesque stone sarcophagus, and in the third chapel on the right the 14th century panel painting of *Our Lady of the Rains.* Observe the fine wooden pulpit and the beautiful choir made of the same material.

CEMETERY
Vyšehradský hřbitov

Originally a medieval cemetery adjoining the **Church of St Peter and St Paul**, it was transformed into a **memoria**l of Czech art and culture in the latter half of the 19th century. Famous figures buried here include the painter M. Aleš, the writers K. Čapek, B. Němcová and J. Neruda, and the composers A. Dvořák and B. Smetana. The sculptors B. Kafka, J. V. Myslbek and L. Šaloun are buried in the *Slavín Chapel.*

The funerary monument to Antonín Dvořák.

Opposite page: the monument to Jan Neruda and on the right, the Pantheon, topped by the Spirit of the Country; below the tomb of Bedřich Smetana.

A view of the Monumental Cemetery, with the Pantheon (Slavin) in the background. The Pantheon was built in 1890 to celebrate the nation's glories and heroes.

Žižkov

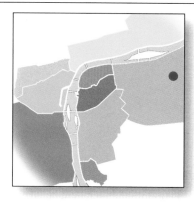

Žižkov Tower
Žižkovská věž

Erected between 1985 and 1992, this modern tower has quickly become a landmark on the city's skylines. Designed by the architects V. Aulický and J. Kozák, the steel structure soars to a height of 216 metres. In addition to supplying the city's radio and TV signals, it offers a splendid view of Prague and its surroundings. An elevator takes visitors to the panoramic terrace and restaurant.

Church of the Sacred Heart
Kostel nejsvětějšího srdce Páně

In the middle of *Jiřího z Poděbrad* Square is the modern Church of the Sacred Heart, designed by the architect Josip Plečnik and erected between 1928 and 1932. The building, with a single nave, inspired by early Christian basilicas, is made of brick and granite. The simple **interior** has a coffered ceiling and a marble altar dominated by the statues of *Christ and the Bohemian Saints,* by the sculptors D. Pešan and B. Stefan. The huge clock on the facade is reminiscent of the rose windows on Gothic cathedrals.

A detail of the monumental, modern Church of the Sacred Heart.

The impressive Žižkov Tower soars to a height of 216 metres and offers a magnificent view of the city. The "Children" (one is shown here) are by David Černý and were added after the tower was completed. The faces, transformed into bar codes, express strong criticism of our era.

Holešovice

The Dancing Fountain (*Křižíkova Fontána*), stands in front of the modern pavilion of the Prague fair and offers a truly unusual sight: jets of water among colourful lights dance to the rhythms of interesting music.

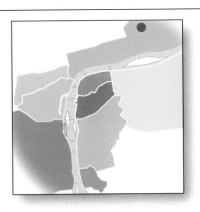

Troja

The magnificent double baroque staircase adds yet another elegant touch to the façade of Troja Palace.

TROJA PALACE
Trojský zámek

This splendid Baroque palace ranks among the most beautiful summer residences in the capital. It is situated in the quarter of Troja, which lies to the north of the Vltava, in the northern suburbs of Prague. The architect G. B. Mathey was commissioned to build the palace by Count Sternberg, one of the best-known members of the city's aristocracy. Mathey completed the building between 1679 and 1685, modelling the exterior on the style of the classical Italian villa. The magnificent staircase which leads down to the garden was added between 1685 and 1703. It has a double flight of steps and is decorated with mythological statues by Johann Georg, Paul Hermann, and the Brokoff brothers (*Sons of Mother Earth, Struggle between the Olympian Gods and the Titans*). Inside the building note the great **Imperial Hall**, decorated with beautiful frescoes by A. Godin showing the *Glory of the Habsburgs*. This Dutch artist, who worked on the hall's decoration, also painted the noteworthy *Personification of Justice*. The so-called **Chinese Rooms** contain a collection of ceramics and are decorated with 19th-century wall paintings of Chinese scenes. The palace, which because of its imposing nature is also known as *Troja Castle*, is complemented by the beautiful and enchanting **Troja Gardens.** These were designed by the architect Mathey, who in fact planned the entire complex; he made the gardens in a distinctly early-French Baroque style. From the *Orangeries* at the bottom of the gardens, not far from the Vltava, there is a charming view of the whole of this miniature Bohemian 'Versailles'.

Careful restoration work has returned the Troja palace and gardens to their former splendour. The palace contains a 19th century art collection.

INDEX

Introduction 3

The districts
Holešovice 141
Hradčany 34
Josefov 108
Letenské Sady 71
Malá Strana 50
Nové Město 120
Smíchov 72
Staré Město 84
Troja 142
Vyšehrad 133
Žižkov 140

Archbishop's Palace 35
Astronomical Clock..................97
Beer Museum 128
The Castle 6
Black Tower 31
Castle Gardens 32
    Royal gardens 33
    South Gardens 32
Cathedral of St Vitus 14
- The Interior 20
    The Cathedral Treasury
    and the Crown Jewels 24
    The Chapel
    of St Wenceslas 25
    The Chapels 22
    The Rotunda 24
- South façade 19
- West façade 18
The Changing of the Guard ..10
Chapel of the Holy Cross 12
First Courtyard 8
Giants' Gate 8
Golden Lane 30
Lobkowicz Palace 30
Masaryk, Tomáš Garrigue 9
Matthias' Gate 10
National Gallery
    in Prague 29
North Wing: Rudolph Gallery
    and Spanish Hall 12
Royal Palace 26
    The interior 26
Second Courtyard 11
St George's Monastery and
    Basilica 28
Third Courtyard 13

Celetná Street 104
Cemetery 138
Charles Bridge 74
    Statues on the Charles Bridge... 78
Charles IV 84
Charles Square 129
Charles Street 92
Church of Our Lady
    of the Snows 121
Church of Our Lady of Týn 99
Church of Our Lady Victorious 68
Church of Saint John
    of Nepomuk 45
Church of Saint John
    on the Rock 130
Church of Saint Mary
    and Charlemagne 129
Church of Saint Mary
    and the Slavonic Patrons
    (Na Slovanech Monastery) 130
Church of St Francis Seraphicus at
    the Knights of the Cross 85
Church of St James 105
Church of St Lawrence 71
Church of St Nicholas in Malá
    Strana 63
Church of St Nicholas in Staré
    Město 103
Church of St Peter
    and St Paul 136
Church of St Thomas 69
Church of the
    Annunciation 130
Church of the Holy Saviour 86
Church of the Nativity
    (The Loreto) 41
Church of the Sacred Heart 140
Clam-Gallas Palace 92
Clementinum 87
Czernin Palace 37
Dvořák Museum 131
Estates Theatre 104
Goltz-Kinský Palace 102
High Synagogue 114
House 'at the Golden Unicorn' 100
House 'at the Stone Bell' 102
Hradčany Square 34
Jewish Museum 110
Jindřišská Tower 121
Jubilee Synagogue 122
Kafka, Franz 110
Kampa Island 68
Klausen Synagogue 115

Knight of the Cross Square 84
Kolowratský Palace 53
Little Quarter Square 53
The Loreto 39
    Church of the Nativity 41
    Cloister 40
    Santa Casa Chapel 39
    Treasury 40
Maisel Synagogue 116
Martinitz Palace 34
Mirror Maze 70
*Monument to the Victims of
Communism* 71
*Monument to the Victims of the
Resistance* 71
Mozart Museum 72
Municipal House 105
Na Příkopě Street 120
National Gallery
    in Prague...............29, 36, 106
National Museum of Prague ...125
National Theatre 126
Nerudova Street........................52
New World 44
Observatory 71
Old Jewish Cemetery 111
Old Town Hall 96
Old Town Square 94
Old-New Synagogue 112
The Palace Gardens beneath
    the Castle 59
Petřín Observation Tower 70
Pinkas Synagogue 117
Powder Tower 104
Rudolfinum -
    House of Artists 107
Saint John of Nepomuk 44
Schwarzenberg Palace 35
Smetana Museum 90
Spanish Synagogue 118
St Agnes' Convent 106
Sternberg Palace 36
Storch House 100
Strahov Monastery 46
Troja Palace 142
Tuscan Palace 35
Villa Amerika 131
Villa Betramka 72
Vrtba Palace 67
Vyšehrad Park 134
Wallenstein Palace 54
Wenceslas Square 120
Žižkov Tower 140